CW00524782

THE CAIRO
EISTEDDFOD

THE CAIRO EISTEDDFOD

and other Welsh adventures in Egypt

Ivor Wynne Jones

ISBN: 0-86381-830-7

Cover design: Sian Parri

First published in 2003 by
Gwasg Carreg Gwalch, 12 Iard yr Orsaf, Llanrwst,
Wales LL26 0EH
℡ 01492 642031 🖹 01492 641502
✆ books@carreg-gwalch.co.uk   website: www.carreg-gwalch.co.uk

Contents

Hiraeth in Cairo

In the midst of World War II some 200 Welsh soldiers, sailors and airmen assembled in Cairo to hear a corporal ask: *A oes heddwch?* – i.e. 'Is there peace'. Back came the enthusiastic reply: *Heddwch!* ('Peace!'). To strangers outside, in Maruf Street, it would have sounded like a call to mutiny – if they could understand Welsh – but the servicemen had merely taken a few hours off from war to convene the first Cairo Eisteddfod. Some of them had managed to find military transport from as far away as the northern extremity of Palestine, which was then a British state, ruled under a League of Nations mandate stitched up by Britain's Welsh Prime Minister David Lloyd George, out of the victories of World War I.

The date was Saturday 25 September, 1943. All German and Italian resistance in North Africa had ended on 13 May, when the American Task Force and British 1st Army from the west, and General Montgomery's 8th Army from Egypt linked up in Tunisia. On 9 July British and American forces landed in Sicily, and on 9 September they began the invasion of Italy.

Thus by August of 1943 Cairo, with its enormous garrison, had become something of a military backwater, apart from the multitude of secret intelligence units that had always used the city to survey events from the Indian Ocean to the Mediterranean. Flying Officer T. Elwyn Griffiths, from

Llandybie, was serving with one such unit, in the photographic interpretation section at RAF Heliopolis – now Cairo International Airport. It was from his tiny RAF office that he was able to turn his attention to the activities of the Middle East Welsh Societies that had sprung up in Cairo, Alexandria, Kasfareet, Jerusalem, Haifa and Abadan. Veterans dispute which came first. A St. David's Day programme by the Jerusalem society was broadcast as early as 1941, but only three Welshmen were present: Dillwyn Miles (from Pembrokeshire), Iorwerth Jones (Llangefni) and Richard Hughes (Betws-y-coed), who had lived in Palestine since 1890. *Bugeilio'r gwenith gwyn* was sung by an Arab tenor, in acceptable Welsh, to the accompaniment of a harp played by a Palestinian Jew. That was also the year in which both the Alexandria and Cairo veterans claim to have been the pioneers of properly structured Middle East Welsh societies.

Whatever its position in the 1941 pecking order, Cymdeithas Gymreig Alecsandria was formed while the ancient Mediterranean harbour was the base for the abortive British campaign in Greece, and the temporary success by the army pushing the Italians west across Libya. By 1 July, 1942, however, German Field Marshal Erwin Rommel's *Afrika Korps* was only 70 miles down the road from Alexandria, at El Alamein. That day was long remembered in Cairo as 'Ash Wednesday', a reference to the clouds of ash that rose high above the city, aided by the summer heat, as the British administration burned mountains of secret documents in danger of falling into German hands.

Oddly, there was never any 'black out' in Cairo – the practice of obscuring all lights at night so as to confuse enemy bombers – because no bombers headed for Cairo, not even an enemy reconnaissance plane. There was no food rationing in this seething Nile metropolis, and the shops remained full, while hotels and bars flourished like never before. So did the brothels, at 5 piastres a time (half a soldier's daily pay, equating with today's five UK pence), the service coming complete with a free 'French letter' (condom) and tube of antiseptic ointment, by courtesy of the Royal Army Medical Corps orderly at the door of approved establishments – the rest all displaying a large 'out of bounds' sign (a red saltire in a circle), fixed at the entrance by the Military Police.

Military clubs, spanning all the Commonwealth and Allied components of the huge garrison, sprouted in the city centre, where there was no shortage of fuel for cheap taxis to a wide variety of entertainment. The reason for Cairo's carnival atmosphere was simple: despite the battles raging on its land a few miles north of Cairo, Egypt was neutral! Under British pressure Egypt broke off diplomatic relations with Germany on 3 September, 1939, and the Nazi ambassador was sent home, but otherwise King Faruk regarded himself as living in peace with Adolf Hitler, and was suspected of living in hope of a German victory, so as to get the British off his back. The war was nearly over, with British troops already on the Rhine, before Faruk declared war in February 1945, and only then so as to earn his country a seat among the victors in the new

United Nations Organisation. The revenge of soldiers based in Egypt was simple: prompted by two or three *Stella* beers, or the formal end to a cinema performance, they would sing a ribald mixture of English and Arabic lyrics, saying the foulest things about King Faruk and Queen Farida, to the tune of the Egyptian National Anthem that had been written by Verdi.

Soldiering on the Nile was nothing new to the men of Wales. To this day the Royal Regiment of Wales (24th/41st Foot) incorporates the Sphinx of Giza in its badges. This is a reminder that one of its constituent regiments, the South Wales Borderers (24th Foot), together with the Royal Welch Fusiliers (23rd Foot), who display the Sphinx on their Colours, earned the battle honour 'Egypt' during the 1801-02 campaign to drive out the army of Napoleon Bonaparte. France had occupied Egypt since 1798, and the graffiti of Napoleon's troops can still be seen on some of the country's ancient monuments as far south as Abu Simbel. After expelling the French the British troops withdrew, resulting in a period of anarchy until 1805, when Muhammad Ali, commanding an Ottoman army regiment of Albanians, was invited by a deputation of Cairo citizens to seize power and restore order. That led to his notorious massacre, in 1811, of 470 leaders of the dominant Mamluks (feudal professional soldiers trained from childhood) who had been invited to a banquet at Cairo citadel. Under the command of his son Ibrahim Pasha, Muhammad Ali's French-officered army extended Egyptian control across Arabia, south into Sudan and northeast into Syria and Anatolia. In

1839 he turned on the Ottomans and captured their fleet. It was Egypt's greatest hour, but was short-lived. With shades of the 2003 Middle East politics of US president George Bush and UK prime minister Tony Blair, Muhammad Ali was suddenly declared to be a threat to European interests, and by 1841 the Egyptian ruler's only imperial province was the Sudan, after Turkey had been persuaded to restore Ottoman military control in the rest of its sprawling empire.

Muhammad Ali was succeeded in 1848 by his grandson Abbas Pasha, as ruling viceroy for the Ottoman Empire. His reign was largely devoted to reversing the Westernising reforms of his grandfather. Next came the viceroys Said Pasha (1854-63) and Ismail Pasha (1863-79), and the opening of the Suez Canal in 1863 to consolidate British interest in the country. In the same way as medieval Welsh princes had maintained some independence by paying tribute to the reigning king of England, so Ismail paid tribute to the Ottomans, for which he was awarded the impressive title of Khedive (Lord) of Egypt in 1867. Heavy borrowing forced him to sell his Suez Canal shares to the British government in 1875. Both Egypt's and the Khedive's finances were placed under international control in 1878, when Ismail was also forced to include Europeans in his ruling cabinet.

For the first, but not the last time, the Egyptian army officer corps, led by Colonel Ahmad Arabi, rebelled in 1881 against the Khedive and growing foreign influence. Subsequent unrest resulted in the arrival of the British and French navies off Alexandria in May

1882, and serious street rioting in June, when many Christians were murdered for no other reason than sharing the religion of the non-Islamic enemy. British warships began bombarding the city in July, and on the 13th Colonel Arabi declared war on Britain. Two days later the Khedive asked for British protection, and the Ottoman Sultan, in Constantinople, outlawed Arabi. That brought back the British army, ostensibly to uphold the authority of the Khedive. Cairo Citadel, the ancient centre of administration, was captured on 14 September, 1882, and thereafter the British army stayed for three-quarters of a century.

Just a year later Samuel Evans, who began his working life as a journalist at the old *Herald* Office, in Caernarfon's Castle Square, went to Cairo on being appointed private secretary to Edgar Vincent, whom the British had appointed financial adviser to the Khedive they had restored to *de jure* control. At least that is what it was meant to look like, but only so long as the Khedive obeyed London. Samuel Evans was born in 1858, the son of Richard Evans, farmer of Pant-y-garn, Rhiwabon. He was 20 when he began reporting for *Yr Herald Cymraeg* and the *Caernarvon & Denbigh Herald*. After two years in Caernarfon he moved to the *Sheffield Independent*, from where he was selected in 1883 for colonial service in Cairo. In 1887 he was given command of the Egyptian Coastguards, which was the nearest thing to a navy allowed to the Khedive. In 1889 Edgar Vincent was appointed governor of the Ottoman Bank, in Constantinople (now Instanbul), and he asked Evans to accompany him, as secretary general of the bank. From Constantinople Evans travelled widely, promoting the bank's interests in places as far as Baghdad and Teheran – where, in 1894, the Shah gave him a new job as head of Persia's tobacco industry, for which the general secretary was Ellis Jones Griffiths, from Anglesey. In 1895 Griffiths left Teheran to become Liberal MP for Anglesey. When Vincent left Constantinople in 1896, for a new job in South Africa, he again asked Samuel Evans to join him. Thus Evans emigrated for the last time. He became civil commissioner for Johannesburg after the Boer War, and in 1909 was appointed chairman of the Crown Gold Mines, a job he retained until his death in 1935.

Samuel Evans appears to have been the first Welshman to establish a career in Cairo. His influence on Nile society was to be seen from 1886 until 1956, including the 1943 Cairo Eisteddfod. Furthermore his influence might be said to live on in today's Wales International, the World-wide society formerly known as Undeb y Cymry ar Wasgar (Union of Welsh People in Dispersion), and its journal *Yr Enfys* ('The Rainbow') that was born out of Cairo's World War II *Seren y Dwyrain* ('Star of the East').

Cairene Cofis

Samuel Evans was a cousin of the truly remarkable Bryan brothers, of Cairo, usually regarded as Caernarfon Cofis, although they were born at

Camddwr, Llanarmon-yn-Iâl, the sons of Edward and Elinor Bryan. When still young children, the family moved to a remote holding at Cyrn y Brain, above Dyffryn Maelor. They attended schools at Llanarmon, Minera and Wrexham. John Davies Bryan was the second to be born, but effectively the eldest because the firstborn died when only six months old. He derived what later became his famous middle name – still shown as recently as 2002 on the street maps of Cairo – from John Davies, of Nercwys, a relative of his mother. As a youth he was apprenticed to a Mostyn Quay draper, Enoch Lewis, father of Sir J. Herbert Lewis who served as a Liberal MP from 1892 to 1922. He moved on to a sequence of two shops in Liverpool, where he developed chest problems. That prompted him to leave the smoke and dust-laden city to manage the famous Afr Aur (Golden Goat) drapery shops, owned by Pierce & Williams, on opposite corners of Eastgate Street, in Caernarfon's Turf Square (and later one on the corner of Turf Square and Bridge Street, after Lloyd's Bank had taken over one of the shops, which they altered and retained until 2002).

In 1883 John was joined by his brother Edward, to open their own general drapery and millinery shop, labelled as Bryan Brothers, at 12 Bridge Street, Caernarfon, making their home above the shop next door, at No.10. John Davies Bryan was still in ill health when Samuel Evans revisited the *Caernarfon Herald* of his youth in 1885, and suggested his cousin might benefit from winters spent in the more amenable climate of Egypt. John set off in 1886, liked what he saw, and opened a store stocked with British goods within part of the Continental Hotel, in Shari Emad ad-Din, the Oxford Street of Cairo. He claimed to be Cairo's first fixed-price shopkeeper, marking all his goods with a figure that was not open to the long-winded haggling, bluff and counter-bluff that was part of the ingrained Egyptian culture. The business was a great success and brother Joseph, a student at Aberystwyth, left the university in 1887 to join the Cairo enterprise.

John visited Caernarfon in 1888, when it was agreed to sell the shop in Bridge Street, so that Edward could run a new branch of Davies Bryan & Co., which they would open in Alexandria. Alas, within a fortnight of their arrival in Cairo John was struck down with typhoid fever, and died on 13 November, aged 33. He was buried in the old Protestant cemetery at the foot of the Mokatam hills (source of the stone for the pyramids of Giza). John was the first of the four brothers to be buried in Egypt, followed by Robert in 1920 (in Cairo), Edward in 1929 (in Alexandria's Chatby cemetery) and Joseph in 1935 (in Alexandria). Catherine, wife of Edward, was buried in Alexandria in 1921. (Joseph's wife Jane was buried in Aberystwyth in 1930).

Robert Bryan, the poet and musician, was born in 1858. He was educated at Wrexham British School and Bangor Normal College, and became a teacher, first at Corwen and later at Talysarn. He then matriculated to Aberystwyth University College, where he spent just one term before moving on to Oxford. His health broke in 1893, before he was able to sit for his degrees of BA and Mus.Bac. He ostensibly settled at Marchwiel, Wrexham, until 1903 when he moved to Caernarfon, but actually spent most of his time in Egypt, believing the climate to be better for his health. He published a volume of poetry, *Odlau Cân*, in 1901, and composed a lot of music, one of his most popular pieces being *Y Teithiwr Blin*, for male choirs. He is named as the translator of Wordsworth's *Ode to immortality*, for the Welsh duet *Gwyll a Gwawl*, believed to have been first sung in 1899. His, too, are the modern words for the famous lullaby *Suo Gân*, rescued and embellished from an old manuscript. The second and third verses of *Y Gwcw Fach* are by Robert Bryan, and it was he who edited *Alawon y Celt* (1904-05). Despite spending most of his adult life with his brothers in Egypt he took no part in the business.

After John's death Edward and Joseph established their Alexandria branch in an impressive three-bay five-storey building in Shari Sharif Pasha or, as it was more usually called, in deference to the port's large and influential French and Greek population, Rue Sharif Pasha – named after the man who led the first British-controlled Egyptian government after the 1882 invasion. This was one of the most commercially advantageous sites in town, and London-Welsh architect Robert Williams was commissioned to replace an earlier building with a façade of red Aberdeen granite and stone quarried in Somerset. The national symbols of leek, rose, shamrock and thistle were carved into the stonework – and the building still stands.

Among Edward Bryan's subsequent Alexandria

neighbours, in Rus el-Rasafa, was born a Welshman-by-proxy who is never likely to be given a place in *Y Bywgraffiadur Cymreig* (Dictionary of Welsh Biography). He was Rudolf Hess, born in 1894, eventually to become Deputy Führer of Nazi Germany, before spending most of World War II as a prisoner at Y Fenni *(Abergavenny)*, to die as the last of the war criminals incarcerated at Spandau military prison, in Berlin. He was the son of former Cardiff schoolteacher Carl Hess, whose first wife lies buried beside the path leading to the door of Llanfihangel-y-fedw church.

The Cairo shop was extended into the ground floor of Grand Continental Hotel Buildings, an impressive seven-bay four-storey structure. By 1909 they had acquired a site that enabled them to move along the street, where they built St. David's Buildings, fronting on to Shari Emad ad-Din, and stretching south to the corner of Shari el-Manak (later called Shari Malika Farida, after King Faruk's first Queen, and now Shari Abd-al Khalik Tharwat, in honour of the prime minister of Egypt's 1922 government). It was to become the most famous department store in the Middle East. After the Battle of Omdurman, in 1898, an Anglo-Egyptian agreement was signed for the joint rule of Sudan, and by the end of the 19th century Davies Bryan & Co. had opened a third shop, in Khartoum. A fourth was to follow at Port Said, and a fifth in London.

With the outbreak of World War I, in 1914, Britain unilaterally ended Egypt's status as a province of the Ottoman Empire and declared it to be a British protectorate, which was just one diplomatic step short of being annexed as a colony – although that was what the country had been, effectively, since 1882. In 1917 Britain installed the European-educated non-Arabic-speaking autocratic Fuad as Egypt's Sultan, effectively the first king since the days of the pharaohs. The United States promptly recognised the British Protectorate, to the despair of Egyptian nationalists.

During World War I the Bryan brothers made it known that Welsh soldiers would find a welcome cup of coffee at their shops, where there was always an especially warm response to Welsh speakers. Their hospitality was enhanced by the enthusiasm of their principal Cairo salesman, Robert Hughes, a young man born in Cricieth in 1890. He was the husband of Elizabeth Ellen, who was the daughter of Ruth (originally of Denbigh) and Lewis Williams (of Pencaenewydd). Ruth had a brother, William Jones, a grocer who lived in Dinorwig Street, Caernarfon, a few yards from the Vaynol Road home of Edward Bryan. William Jones married Alice, sister of Nell, the wife of Edward Bryan. Elizabeth Ellen's half-brother Edward Roberts was already working for Davies Bryan, thus the expanded family found a job in Cairo for Robert Hughes, because of his ill health: he sailed from Swansea on 12 October, 1915, aboard the SS *Fabian*, for what he described in his unpublished diary as 'my first journey abroad'. One of the first Welsh soldiers he greeted in Cairo, on 8 March, 1916, was his brother Eliseus Hughes.

His name keeps cropping up in the Orient, although now confused with another Robert Hughes, a

Welshman who ran his own shoe business in Cairo, but about whom nothing seems to be known. We know there were two men of the same name from a letter written by Edward Bryan in November 1909, referring to the impending construction of their new St David's Building on a three-quarter acre site *'ar gyfer yr Eastern Telegraph Co., rhan ohono yn ein heol ni, a rhan yn heol lle roedd Robert Hughes ynddo'*. i.e. partly in the road of John Davies Bryan's first shop and partly around the corner, where Robert Hughes had a shop, seemingly in Shari el-Manak. Robert Hughes's shoe shop was listed as one of those destroyed by arsonists in 1952. Malaria forced Robert Hughes, the Davies Bryan salesman, to leave Egypt and he returned to Cricieth, where he died in 1947, aged 56. One of his best-remembered customers was Tremadog-born Thomas Edward Lawrence, later to earn fame as Lawrence of Arabia.

Britain terminated Egypt's protectorate status in 1922 and, without any bilateral negotiation, elevated Fuad from Sultan to King, and declared his country to be an independent kingdom, but subject to British 'reservation' of control in many spheres of the country's national sovereignty and international affairs. After World War I Edward Bryan bought Crug, now the Judges' Lodgings, outside Caernarfon, and he spent a lot of time there on long visits to escape the summer heat of Egypt. He died in 1929, leaving a £52 a year pension to his Crug housekeeper, Ellen Hughes. His other bequests included £500 each to the Calvinistic Methodist Forward Movement in Wales and the Calvinistic Methodist Aged Ministers' Fund; £200 to the British & Foreign Bible Society; and £500 to the University College of Wales, Aberystwyth, to provide a fund to perpetuate the Robert Bryan Musical Scholarship. He left £100,000 – an enormous sum at that time – in trust for his daughter Olwen Hilton-Jones, and £15,000 to his grandson Bryan Hilton-Jones, then aged 12.

Joseph Bryan, by then the last of the four brothers, soon decided to sell the family business, giving the first option to Fred Purslow, of Wrexham, who had been living in Cairo since 1918. Mr Purslow bought only the older half of the Cairo shop, retaining as his address the name Davies Bryan Building, but trading as 'Purslow, English draper', advertising 'outfitting, shirts, ties, underwear, dressing gowns, pyjamas.'

The Anglo-Egyptian Treaty of 1936 was negotiated against the background of the British military suppression of the Arab revolt in neighbouring Palestine, in protest against the greatly increased Jewish immigration arising out of Nazi Germany's xenophobia. The treaty was designed to strengthen Egyptian sovereignty. It stipulated close co-operation in the event of war, and a 20-year programme of improving Egypt's self-defence, to the point where British troops could be withdrawn to the Suez Canal Zone. The Egyptian Military Academy was opened to a broader range of citizens – and its first graduates under the new regime included two future Egyptian presidents, Gamal abd an-Nasir (abd el-Nasser) and Anwar Sadat. At the request of Britain, Egypt was admitted to the League of Nations in 1937.

Business was booming in Shari Emad ad-Din. Egypt's new elite, and the growing legion of foreign diplomats to the newly independent kingdom, all discovered the Welsh reputation for quality and fair trade established by Davies Bryan & Co, and patronised Fred Purslow's St David's Buildings. So did the increasing flow of tourists attracted by the romance of the Nile, and the commercial future looked exceedingly bright.

With the outbreak of World War II Fred Purslow, like Edward Bryan a quarter of a century earlier, opened his house to Welsh servicemen passing through the city, and he was quick to subsidise what developed into today's Wales International.

With five years of the Anglo-Egyptian Treaty still to run, Egypt unilaterally abrogated it in October 1951. In January 1952 crowds took to the streets of Cairo (in response to a Canal Zone skirmish the previous day, when British troops killed 50 Egyptian policemen) and set fire to 700 buildings symbolising British rule and commerce. Twelve people were killed and thrown into the flames of the exclusive Turf Club; the famous Shepheard's Hotel, Groppi's restaurant, Barclays Bank, the Opera Cassino, Rivoli cinema, Thomas Cook's, the offices of the British Council and the British Institute, shops, bars and nightclubs, and motor car showrooms were all destroyed or seriously damaged. St David's Buildings was looted and damaged, but eventually reopened. Hard on the heels of the riots a group from the Egyptian army officer corps, led by Colonel Nasser, rebelled against the government of King Faruk, expelled him, and soon afterwards installed General Muhammad Neguib as first president of the new republic.

Two years later Nasser challenged Neguib and took over the presidency. He negotiated an agreement for the British army to leave a country it had occupied for 72 years, although arrangements were made for Britain to maintain some control of the Suez Canal, with civilian contractors looking after military bases and stores that would become quickly available to the British army in the event of a Cold War emergency.

In July 1956 however, Nasser nationalised the Canal. Fred Purslow was on holiday at Coedpoeth at the time, and it was there that he learnt of the revolutionary government's ban on the sale of British goods – the very goods on which his shop had established its reputation. He had already decided there was little point in trying to maintain the business founded by John Davies Bryan seventy years earlier, but worse was to follow. Within days both the shop and the elegant town centre house of Mr & Mrs Purslow, at 6 Shari el-Bustan, together with all its splendid oriental contents, were confiscated without compensation.

Israel invaded Egyptian Sinai in October, as part of a secret conspiracy that gave British and French troops an excuse to invade Egypt, ostensibly to protect international shipping rights in the Canal. Britain hoped to resume its 1882-1954 hegemony, while the French, who had been nursing a grievance since 1802, saw an opportunity to avenge Napoleon's defeat at the hands of soldiers of the Royal Welch Fusiliers and the

South Wales Borderers. London and Paris had assumed America would support the 1956 invasion, sparked off by its Israeli client state, but much to the surprise and rapid political demise of prime minister Sir Anthony Eden, the United States supported the Soviet Union in calling for a quick withdrawal of all the invaders.

Eden was at Llandudno, for the Conservative Party's annual conference, when he heard of America's reaction, creating a situation in marked contrast to prime minister Tony Blair's prompt support for America's paranoid meddling in Iraqi affairs in 2003! By a strange twist of history Anthony Eden was the Foreign Secretary who signed the 1936 Anglo-Egyptian Treaty, after which he featured on an Egyptian postage stamp. With shades of the 2003 Iraq crisis, Eden recalled, in his memoirs, that the Soviet veto of the United Nations Security Council Resolution required to bring Nasser to heel, and American talk of a negotiated solution for the Suez problem, left him rewriting his Llandudno speech during what should have been his lunch-break. He said he decided to 'point out once again that force could not be excluded' and to express his concern at the consequences of America's 'unjustified flights of hopeful fancy'.

It was some years later before Fred Purslow was able to obtain a visa to return to Cairo, where he found the once-famous shop of Davies Bryan & Co. had been converted into a warren-like cheap bazaar, by the government of President Nasser. He was refused permission to remove any of his savings from his Cairo bank, and so he shared a sizeable fortune between the members of the staff who had been working for him in 1956 (seventeen of whom became successful businessmen).

That was the end of an honourable chapter in Welsh commercial history, which began when former *Herald Cymraeg* reporter Samuel Evans dined with draper John Davies Bryan above his Caernarfon shop in 1885. Ironically, in a city where street names are frequently changed, and statues are removed, to reflect the politics of the day, the fame of the Welsh shop is such that it is still shown on modern maps and guidebooks as 'Davies Bryan Building', now an apartment block with some shops at street level. Today it is best known for the section housing the Anglo-Egyptian Bookshop, at an address quoted as 156 Shari Muhammad Farid, a continuation of what is still best known to taxi drivers as Shari Emad ad-Din.

Trwsus Ffestin

Items of clothing that would not have been found on the Cairo shelves of Davies Bryan & Co. were *trwsus Ffestin*, meaning 'Ffestin's trousers', yet seventh-century Cairo was the unexpected origin of this peculiar name for the thick off-white cotton trousers favoured by the rockmen of Blaenau Ffestiniog, before the more recent advent of universal American jeans.

Trwsus Ffestin was an understandable colloquial mispronunciation, in the parish dedicated to St. Ffestin, of *trwsus ffystyn*, which became a uniform in the Victorian slate mines, a status symbol of the rockmen, as distinct from the uniform jackets of the same thick material worn by the slate makers. These hardwearing garments were made from fustian, a much-abused word in the English language but which first meant a particular weave of Egyptian linen, which had given us the Latin word *fustaneum.*

Undergoing slight changes as it crossed Europe, the word and material eventually arrived at Ffestiniog as the English fustian, which became the Welsh *ffystyn*, soon corrupted to Ffestin, for what was by then American cotton rather than Egyptian linen. In modern Cairo the word for a woman's dress is *fustan.* All are derived from Al-Fustat, the original Cairo, founded south of the present city in 642 AD, as the garrison for the newly arrived Arab conquerors of Egypt, who incorporated the earlier Byzantine Roman fortified town of Babylon.

Egyptian scholars cannot agree on the origin of the garrison's name. The obvious explanation is *fustat*, an alternative Arabic name for 'tent' (more usually 'chaima'). However papyri suggest that before the Arabs arrived Babylon had become known as Fossaton – a Latin-Greek name meaning 'fosse'. A fosse, or moat, surrounded Babylon, giving added defence and much-needed drainage of what is still a wet area, with a high water plane, on the banks of the Nile.

It was at Al-Fustat that the inhabitants of Egypt's first Islamic town began weaving their durable ribbed linen, which became widely used throughout the

Mediterranean during the Middle Ages. Old Fustat still stands, fenced off but virtually abandoned to a resident caretaker and a policeman, and an occasional archaeological dig by the American University in Cairo. It has given its name to the neighbouring suburb of Fustat which, as well as claiming to have the oldest church in Egypt (the Coptic Orthodox St Sergius) also houses the New Protestant Cemetery, beside Shari Salah Salem.

There one can find many Welsh graves, like that of Captain Thomas Henry Jones, of the Merchant Navy, beloved husband of Florence, born at New Quay, Cardiganshire, in 1894, and who died at Ras Gharib in 1941. Who was Captain Trefor Jones, also of the Merchant Navy, who died in 1942, aged 48? Or Gwen, daughter of John and Annie Jones, who died in 1932, aged 24? What of Percy Thomas Jones, who died in Cairo in 1939, aged 50? Then there is Jessie Jean, widow of Arthur Trevor Williams, who died in the city in 1937, aged 60. Next to her is the grave of Sarah Helen, wife of G.E. Evans, who died in 1937, aged 61.

In the adjacent British Military Cemetery lie hundreds of the Territorial Army volunteers of the 53rd Welsh Division, who set out to liberate Palestine from the Turks in the Last Crusade, which spanned 31 years from 1917 to 1948 – many of them dying of nasty diseases or accidents before setting foot in the Holy Land. Among them we find Captain Trevor R. Allaway, MC, of Artro House, Llanbedr, Merionnydd (his stone mistakenly naming him as Thomas), killed in an accident while serving with the South Wales

Borderers in June 1916.

The remaining headstones give no indication of residence, but they include Royal Welch Fusiliers 41 Ellis W. Jones, of Berriew, 81 John Foulkes, of Bangor, 57 John Williams, of Moelfre, Denbigh, and many others of the 6th Caernarvonshire & Anglesey and 7th Merioneth & Montgomery Battalions, whose RWF cap badge seems to dominate row upon row of well-kept graves, in the only green field for many miles around. Many of these Territorial Army Fusiliers would have begun their soldiering in the pre-war Quarry Company of the regiment – volunteers from the mines and quarries who would have worn *trwsus Ffestin* in Blaenau Ffestiniog before they donned the khaki drill shorts in which they ended their days at Fustat.

There are 2,057 World War I graves and 340 from World War II in the New Protestant Cemetery. Most died in one of the Cairo military hospitals, many from wounds received elsewhere. In 1941 it became necessary to open a new Commonwealth War Graves Commission cemetery beside Shari Nabil el Wakkard, at Heliopolis, northeast of Cairo city centre, where 1,950 are buried.

Singing on the Nile

One of the best known compositions of Robert Bryan, both words and music, is *O Dad Gwroniaid*, published by W.A. Lewis, Liverpool, but with no printed date. It was dedicated to 'Côr Meibion Cymreig Alexandria' (Alexandria Welsh male voice choir), a reminder that several Welsh choirs were formed in Egypt during World War I.

The 53rd Welsh Division arrived at Alexandria in December 1915, after its mauling at the hands of the Turks in the futile Gallipoli campaign. Its units were soon distributed from El Alamein, on the Mediterranean coast, to Fayum, south of Cairo, and Port Suez at the southern end of the Canal. Divisional headquarters was established in the Cairo suburb of Abbasiya, then a concentration of lush gardens surrounding the palatial homes of the ruling wealthy, but now a tatty zone of apartment blocks. In March 1916 the 53rd Welsh Division became part of the new Egyptian Expeditionary Force, or EEF, together with the 52nd Lowland Division, 54th East Anglian Division, and 74th Yeomanry Division, to which were later added the 10th Irish Division and 60th London Division. The Yeomanry Division was made up of pre-war cavalry volunteers of the Territorial Army who had been converted to infantry battalions, incorporating the Denbighshire Yeomanry, Montgomery Yeomanry & Welsh Horse Lancers, Pembroke & Glamorgan Yeomanry, and Shropshire & Cheshire Yeomanry.

In May 1916 the Welsh Division moved to new defensive positions along the length of the Suez Canal. They crossed the Canal in January 1917 to march into Sinai, for what they began to describe as the Ninth Crusade. Months later, after such battles as Gaza and

Beersheba, the men began entering Palestine. They wrote home with enthusiasm about the places about which they had heard so much in their chapels and Sunday schools, but their letters were reaching Wales with frustrating deletions. Some words had been obliterated with the heavy blue pencils of the regimental censors, and it took some time to discover the missing words were all references to crusading. The censors were following orders, having been told such Christian words might offend soldiers of the 20th Indian Infantry Brigade serving with the Division. That simplistic excuse concealed David Lloyd George's opportunist plotting of the fundamental cause of today's political chaos in the Middle East. It was a secret that had to be kept from the scheming French, the ambitious Russians, and more especially the Hashemite warriors led by T.E. Lawrence, of Tremadog.

The Alexandria Welsh Choir, in which Robert Bryan took such an interest, was made up of men posted to Egypt as replacements for casualties in the 53rd Division. According to the researches of the Reverend Eric Ramage it was actually formed on a troop ship, in about September 1916. The *ad hoc* choir's enthusiasm led to their being asked to give concerts on the ship, most of whose passengers were soldiers of English regiments.

Their prowess was spotted in Alexandria by Private Alun R. Williams, of Cwmyglo, a Caernarfon schoolmaster, serving with the Royal Engineers, who obtained his commanding officer's permission to raise a choir of about 40 men, for whom he became the conductor. Robert Bryan attended one of their concerts and subsequently wrote several pieces for them. The choir went on to sing in Cairo and in military hospitals along the Nile. At one Cairo concert they sang three of Bryan's compositions: *All Well, Never Alone* and *Ferched Cymru*, together with several traditional Welsh songs. The soloists included a Private Parry, a schoolteacher from Penygroes, who had served in Gallipoli with the 6th (Caernarvonshire) Battalion, Royal Welch Fusiliers. Other soloists were named as Private Elias, of Pwllheli, Private A. Jones, of Pontypridd, and Private Joe Harley, from Mold. A matching choir was formed by men of the Welch Regiment, conducted by their chaplain, Lieutenant the Reverend W. Davies, a Nonconformist minister from Aberfan.

The most colourful of the World War I warriors to pass through Cairo was Thomas Edward Lawrence – the future Lawrence of Arabia – posted to the city as an intelligence officer at the Arab Bureau.

Lawrence of Tremadog

The following is the text of a lecture given by the author to the Friends of the Lloyd George Museum, at Llanystumdwy, in April 2002.

One day in 1947 I found myself talking about Lawrence of Arabia to an Howeitat Bedouin chieftain, or family elder, in the desert somewhere north of the ancient port of Al Akaba. In those days Palestine, Transjordan, Egypt and Saudi Arabia all merged into one bleak landscape in that corner of the world.

Although already driven by the incompatible scent of Arabian oil and the clamour of New York Zionist voters, the United States had not, up to then, managed to supplant British influence and relative stability in the Middle East. Neither did we have today's highway from the Red Sea across Jordan to Baghdad, paid for by Saddam Hussein as a military supply route for the Soviet Bloc armaments that were used to fight Iran, Kuwait and Iraq's own Kurds in the north, and the Shi-ite Marsh Arabs in the south.

Half-a-century ago our occasional military expeditions from Jerusalem or Amman were along ancient dusty tracks, and when we came across a remote encampment of hospitable Bedouin it would have been impolite, even aggressive, if we did not stop to exchange friendly pleasantries in a mixture of Arabic and English. On this particular day in 1947 the chieftain referred to *chaskari Inglezi* – English soldiers, and asked what part of England I came from. I began explaining I was from a country called Wales and – *Gorau Cymro, Cymro oddi cartref* etc – I told him I was in fact a Welsh soldier.

Normally that is the kind of statement that requires you to draw a sketch map of Britain, to end up, at best, protesting you are not Irish. To my amazement the Bedouin said: 'From Captain Lawrence's country', and he went on to explain how he had fought with T.E. Lawrence in the advance on Al Akaba in 1917. His reference to Lawrence as a captain was significant. He was reminiscing about the man he knew, a humble captain, not the colonel of later reference books. Lawrence was a mere lieutenant until February of 1917, by which time he had led the Hashemite army out of the Hejaz Shariffiate to join up with the nomadic Howeitat of Sinai.

After Akaba Lawrence was recommended, by Wingate, for the award of the VC for his bravery in penetrating deep into Ottoman territory while knowing there was a £5,000 reward on his head, dead or alive. The recommendation failed on the technicality of no British officer having been present to witness his bravery, and Lawrence was awarded the Distinguished Service Order – which is no mean medal for a mere subaltern. Later that year he was promoted major and admitted as a Companion of the Order of the Bath.

Thus we have a picture of a lonely British Army captain, in Arab dress, trying to explain to a Bedouin warrior in the remoteness of Sinai that he was Welsh, a tribe the Howeitat had almost certainly never heard of. We all know Thomas Edward Lawrence was born at Gorphwysfa, Tremadog. The original record is still preserved at Pwllheli Register Office, telling us he was born on 15 August, 1888, the son of Thomas Lawrence, gentleman, and Sarah Lawrence, née Maden. He was actually born in the early hours of the 16th, but the date is the least important of all the inaccuracies registered on Lawrence's birth certificate, something to which we will return later.

Lawrence was a very young child when he, his

parents and older brother left Tremadog, first to Scotland, and then on to Brittany in 1891, settling in Oxford in 1894. So why did he attach so much importance to his Welsh place of birth? In 1907 he appeared before a panel at Oxford to proclaim he was born a Welshman, and would die a Welshman, and spoke with sufficient conviction to earn himself a Meyricke exhibition to Jesus College.

After being awarded the exhibition, worth £1 a week – equivalent to a good wage in those days – Ned Lawrence took himself off on an extensive intelligence gathering tour of Wales, including such places as Caernarfon, Harlech and Caerffili, and found himself drawn to the archaeology of ancient ruins such as Dinas Brân, at Llangollen, and Tintern Abbey. He was not particularly complimentary. 'After ten days in Wales I ought to be able to sum up all the character, habits, peculiarities, virtues, vices, and other points of the Welsh people,' he wrote in April 1907, in a letter to his mother. 'I am sorry I cannot do this just yet,' he said, adding: 'They seem to me to be rather inquisitive, more dirty, and exceedingly ugly. I am at last discovering where I got my large mouth from; it's a national peculiarity.

'At the same time they appear honest; I have had no extraordinary bills,' added the 18-years-old rebel preparing for university – having been bought out of the Army by his father. His attribution of his big mouth to Tremadog shows the extent to which he was conscious of his Welsh birth.

Let us jump to 1971, when an American collector

paid £10,000 for some Lawrence of Arabia memorabilia that turned up on the Foyles stand, at a three-day International Antiquarian Book Fair, at the Europa Hotel, in London's Grosvenor Square. There were 30 unpublished letters and other documents, including Lawrence's discharge papers from the RAF, only three months before his fatal motorcycle accident in 1935.

It will be remembered that after the post-1918 politicians, notably David Lloyd George, had carved up and colonised the Middle East which Lawrence of Arabia thought he had won back for the Arabs, from the imperialism of the Turks, the disillusioned Lieutenant-Colonel T.E. Lawrence, CB, DSO, BA, sought to hide his identity. He gave false names and ages and enlisted in the lowest ranks in the Tank Corps and the RAF, wearing uniforms devoid of medal ribbons.

The RAF discharge certificate which surfaced in 1971 was coveted by collectors because it recorded, as permanent identification marks, scars on both buttocks. While would-be purchasers debated whether the scars were caused by sadistic Turkish interrogators in Syria or by a Tank Corps friend in Dorset, I was more interested in the recorded details of the allegedly masochistic Aircraftman Shaw's birth. The document showed Aircraftman Thomas Shaw to have been born on the fictitious date of 15 August, 1894, making Lawrence six years younger than he actually was. He was shown as uneducated and not having earned any campaign medals, let alone gallantry awards. While he was at it he could have chosen anywhere his fancy took him for his birthplace. Yet the only true detail in his RAF records was 'Tremadoc, Caernarvon' as his place of birth.

Thus no matter how far he went to hide his identity, by name and date of birth, the one thing Lawrence never changed was his Welsh place of birth. We have to ask why? Remembering my bizarre conversation with an Howeitat Bedouin in 1947, the 1971 sale prompted me to seek an answer – and I discovered that Lawrence of Arabia was more Welsh than he could ever have known.

In December 1988 I was a guest at the National Portrait Gallery, for the opening of an outstanding exhibition celebrating the centenary of Lawrence's birth. There I found myself in conversation with Peter O'Toole and Jeremy Wilson. O'Toole had, of course, played Lawrence in the famous film, *Lawrence of Arabia.* Jeremy Wilson had written the magnificent 256-page catalogue for the exhibition and was then nearing the completion of the first 'authorised' biography of Lawrence, using previously unavailable documents. I told him of my researches, which instantly began to shed light on his own hunch that Lawrence's roots were more Welsh than his place of birth.

In a letter to Mrs George Bernard Shaw, the adult T.E. Lawrence said his family surname had no better foundation than his father's whim. Not so. His father's real name was Thomas Chapman, not the Thomas Lawrence, gentleman, named on the birth certificate. Chapman was still married to Edith, née Rochfort-Boyd, of County Westmeath, in Ireland, who would not have conceded the description of 'gentleman'. It was she who had appointed Sarah Junner as resident nursemaid for their four children, the youngest of whom was born in 1881.

When Sarah's first illegitimate child, Robert, was born, in Dublin, in 1884, she registered her maiden name as Laurence (spelt with a 'u'). Thomas Chapman left home at about that time and moved in with Sarah. One can only conjecture that he was acknowledging his paternity of Robert. By the time the family turned up at Tremadog they had all adopted the name Lawrence, spelt as we now recognise it.

My contention was that the dominant Sarah Junner, herself illegitimate, had obviously adopted the surname of her own unregistered father, John Lawrence. That presumption required some detective work in the Tyne & Wear Archives, Newcastle, with the enthusiastic assistance of Chief Archivist Bruce Jackson.

T.E. Lawrence, who thrived on half-truths, once told Liddell Hart that his mother's parentage was part English and part Scandinavian. If Lawrence thought he was telling the truth I can now say he did not know very much about his mother, who I hope to show was part Scottish and part Welsh.

Lawrence's claim resulted in Desmond Stewart's incorrect statement, in his book *T.E Lawrence*, that Sarah Maden (the surname used exclusively at Pwllheli Register Office) was the illegitimate daughter of a Norwegian father and an English mother. He told us Sarah had been sent from Sunderland, her place of birth, to be brought up by a relation whose low-church Episcopalian ministry took him to various parts of Scotland, including the Hebrides.

It was Richard Aldington, in his controversial 1955 book *Lawrence of Arabia*, who first made the tentative suggestion that the Sarah Maden of Pwllheli Register Office was really Sarah Junner. Quoting the *Dictionary of National Biography* he said Sarah Maden was the daughter of a Sunderland engineer, and was brought up in the Highlands, and later in Skye. He got as far as discovering that no Sarah Maden was registered as having been born anywhere in Britain during 1861 – the year in which the undocumented Sarah Lawrence appeared to have been born. He also found a birth entry in Sunderland for a Sarah Junner, born on 31 August, 1861, the father being described as a 'shipwright journeyman'.

However Richard Aldington did not press his theory very far, possibly because the original Mrs Sarah Lawrence, of 2 Roker Terrace, Sunderland, was still alive – and if our theories are right she would have been Lawrence of Arabia's great-grandmother. My argument, developed from Aldington's suggestion, is that Mrs Sarah Lawrence was the mother of John Lawrence, a ship's carpenter, who impregnated the family house servant Elizabeth Junner, resulting in the birth of a daughter whom Miss Junner called Sarah – after her employer.

Aldington would not have known of letters from T.E. Lawrence to his mother, by then another Sarah Lawrence, that tell us her 1861 birthday was celebrated on 31 August – the day of Sarah Junner's birth – so let us explore the Lawrences of Sunderland. The 1861 census shows the head of the household to be Thomas Lawrence, a 53-years-old Lloyd's Surveyor, born at Swansea. His wife Sarah was aged 50, and born at Chepstow. Their son John was 18, and described as a ship's carpenter. He was also born at Chepstow. There was an 11-years-old daughter called Sarah, like her mother.

An amendment to the head office copy of the annual *Register Book* for Lloyds' surveyors shows the family moved from Chepstow to Sunderland in 1847, on the appointment of Thomas Lawrence, who appears to have been a master mariner. He was shown as 'deceased' in an 1868 amendment. His will shows he died in August, leaving £600 to his wife.

Elizabeth Junner was listed as a 28-years-old resident servant at the home of the Lawrences, and was said to have born in Scotland. She was by then pregnant and later moved out of Roker Terrace to 7 William Street, in one of the poorer parts of Victorian Sunderland, for the last few weeks of her confinement. She registered that address as her daughter's birthplace, and described herself as 'Junner formerly Junner', a very strange construction, seemingly devised to imply she was married. She named the father as John Junner, a shipwright journeyman. The address 7 William Street appears to have been a block of tenements, with 23 residents in the 1861 census, mostly children or shoemakers working for John Smith. One resident was James Robertson, a 24-years-old ship's carpenter, possibly a friend of John Lawrence.

An 1861 trade directory, which appears to have been out of date, lists a grocer named John Junner living at 14 Hamilton Street, on the opposite shore, at Monkwearmouth. He is not shown in the 1861 census. However, ten years earlier the 1851 census shows Jane Junner as head of the household at 14 Hamilton Street, and describes her as the wife of a sea captain, who was presumably at sea on census night. She was accompanied by two children, aged 16 and 13, and was probably the mother of Elizabeth Junner, who would have been 18, and would have left home to work as a domestic servant. I am quite convinced there was no shipwright named John Junner, as named on the birth certificate of T.E. Lawrence's mother. Elizabeth Junner could not return to work for the Lawrences and found a new home for herself and her baby, working as a servant for a clergyman in her native Scotland.

What can we read into all this? I suggest it is simple. The unmarried 28-years-old servant Elizabeth Junner was seduced, or worse, by the 18-years-old son of her employer. She preserved both his Christian name John and his mother's Christian name Sarah when registering the birth of her daughter. Furthermore she also preserved John Lawrence's trade, which she ascribed to the non-existent John Junner on the birth certificate.

By way of further proof of this theory Miss Elizabeth Junner obviously told her daughter the identity of her father. Sarah Junner's childhood and youth had been spent in Scotland. How else would she have adopted the surname Lawrence if her mother had not told her of her true Sunderland origins? When she first used the new surname, in Dublin, in 1884, she misspelled it, presumably because she had never seen it written. This was corrected by the time she got to Tremadog.

To me that suggests she had written to her mother, telling her she was calling herself Laurence. If that were any old name plucked out of the air the misspelling would not have mattered. It looks as though her mother wrote back, giving her the correct spelling. It may sound complex and circumstantial but I am quite satisfied that I have solved the mystery of Lawrence's surname. So is Jeremy Wilson, who has incorporated my theory, with acknowledgement, in his mammoth biography – his copy to me being endorsed 'I hope I got it right!'

What this tells us, of course, is that Lawrence had a Welsh-born grandfather and Welsh-born great-grandparents. Yet it is unlikely that his mother passed on any of this information, for she probably did not know the origin of the Sunderland family she had never met.

Everything points to T.E. Lawrence's having no concept of the origins of his surname. Even if he tried to reconcile the family birth certificates he would find his mother was Miss Junner, of Sunderland, when born, then Miss Junner of Westmeath, in her nursemaid days, but Miss Laurence (with a 'u'), of Dublin, when her first son was born; becoming the unmarried Mrs Lawrence (with a 'w'), née Maden, by the time T.E. Lawrence was born. For the birth of her third son, in Kirkcudbright, her maiden name was shown as Jenner, not Junner, but it had reverted to Junner for her fourth and fifth sons. All a bit baffling.

That name Maden is a real mystery. I would suggest it is no more than a bit of confusion between Lawrence's father and the Pwllheli Registrar, and is probably a misunderstanding of the question: 'Maiden name?' Births, marriages and deaths entries for that period are riddled with errors. My own father, raised at Tremadog Police Station, only a few years later, was one victim of the Registrar's carelessness, or possibly poor hearing.

None of this helps us solve the mystery of why T.E. Lawrence felt it necessary to go around the world proclaiming his Welshness. One of the more bizarre claims for Lawrence's roots was made by the Reverend D. Tecwyn Evans, in his memoirs *Atgofion Cynnar*, published on his retirement in 1950. He stated that Lawrence of Arabia was the grandson of Lawrence Bach, one time conductor of Talsarnau Band. It was a red herring that subsequently found its way into two or three other books. Just to clear the air, a search aided by Ann Rhydderch, at Gwynedd archives, tells us Lawrence Bach was Cornelius Lawrence, a professional bandmaster, born in Wiltshire in 1831, living at Oswestry in 1867, and at 5 Rhydsarn Cottages, Ffestiniog in 1871. He was most certainly not the father of either Sarah Junner or Sir Thomas Chapman.

Against all the odds Thomas Chapman inherited the family baronetcy in 1914, but never used the title. He and Sarah lived out their lives in Oxford as Mr & Mrs

Lawrence, until his death in 1919. His title could not, of course, be handed down to his illegitimate sons. John Lawrence, who I say was T.E. Lawrence's grandfather, returned to his native Wales in 1870 as the 27-years-old Lloyd's Surveyor for North Wales, North West England and the Isle of Man.

Lawrence of Arabia's last brother, Professor Arnold Walter Lawrence, born at Oxford in 1900, spent much of his life defending the reputation of the desert warrior, often in the forewords he was commissioned to write for several books, or in letters to the editors of various newspapers. After seeing Peter O'Toole's portrayal of our Tremadog hero, in the 1962 film *Lawrence of Arabia*, he said: 'Very pretty, but I don't recognise my brother'.

Whether or not T.E. Lawrence was a homosexual masochist does not matter. What does matter, in the present chaos in the Middle East, is the way in which Lawrence was abused by the British Establishment. Volunteering for Army service soon after the outbreak of war, in 1914, he was commissioned into the Royal Artillery. Having learnt Arabic while in the Levant in 1909, studying Crusader castles for his Oxford thesis, and during subsequent archaeological visits, he was very soon posted to the Arab Bureau in Cairo, as an intelligence officer.

He was only a lieutenant when posted from Cairo to Jeddah, in October 1916, as a liaison officer given the task of stimulating the simmering Arab revolt inspired by Prince Hussein of the Hejaz, the strip of Arabia bordering the Red Sea. Albeit under Turkish control,

Hussein was the eccentric ruler of the Hejaz, but more importantly he was a direct descendant of the Prophet Muhammad and hereditary Sharif of Mecca, Guardian of the Three Holy Mosques of Islam. Only the Mecca and Medina mosques were under his jurisdiction. The third much-coveted mosque was the Al Aksa, on the Temple Mount, towering above the Wailing Wall of the Jews in Jerusalem.

Hussein had long dreamed of shaking off the Ottoman yoke, to enable him to create an Arab kingdom embracing what we now know as Saudi Arabia, Jordan, Israel, Lebanon, Syria, Iraq, Kuwait, Oman, Yemen and the Trucial States. Opportunist imperial Britain was quick to endorse this pan-Arab nationalism – or so the politically naive Lawrence thought!

A week after arriving in the Hejaz he met Sharif Hussein's son Faysal, leader of four brothers actively leading the Revolt in the Desert. In March 1917 Lawrence led the Hashemites in a series of attacks on the Hejaz railway, which ran from Medina to Damascus. In Cairo eyes that was his greatest contribution to the Allied war in the Levant, for it tied up 30,000 Turkish troops, trying to protect their vital imperial rail link.

Lawrence had, by then, espoused the Hashemite jihad and its political agenda, and that took him and Faysal's army into Damascus on 3 October, 1918. Anyone taking his history from the 1962 film would be confused, for it virtually omits any reference to non-Arab forces in Middle East events of 1916-18, which

Lawrence described as: 'An Arab war waged and led by Arabs for an Arab aim in Arabia'. He had no reason to believe he and the Hashemite dynasty were fighting for anything else. But dismayed Nuri as-Said, later a nationalist leader in Iraq, said: 'They could have done it without us', as he watched some of General Allenby's 480,000 Commonwealth troops pour into Damascus, to end centuries of Ottoman hegemony in Arabia.

At the end of their Lawrence-led military struggle for an independent pan-Arab kingdom, with its throne in Damascus, the Arab nationalists, politically led by the great-great-grandfather (Sharif Hussein of the Hejaz), of the present King Abd-Allah of Jordan, found alien politicians sharing out the Levant in a cluster of British and French mandates and protectorates. Palestine, Transjordan, Syria, Iraq and Saudi Arabia were created with wholly artificial frontiers, drawn on a map in straight lines, with nothing more scientific than a ruler and a pencil.

Neither the Hashemites nor Lawrence had known anything of Lloyd George's secret tactical commitment to buy American Zionist support for his war by promising to set up a national home for the Jewish Diaspora in a British-ruled Palestine, while giving Damascus to the French. Faysal was evicted from Damascus by the French, and in 1920 was made the puppet ruler of the brand new Hashemite Kingdom of Iraq, whose real rulers were the British High Commissioner and the local commanding officer of the Royal Air Force. His brother Abd-Allah was made Britain's puppet ruler of Transjordan, or what we now call the Hashemite Kingdom Jordan.

Weakened by the dispersal of his warriors to serve the British, in the wake of Lawrence, and to prop up his sons' artificial kingdoms in Iraq and Jordan, Prince Hussein, Sharif of Mecca, saw the rest of his Hashemite army wiped out by the Saudi Arabian tribes in 1919. He was promptly abandoned by the British and lost the whole of his Hejaz by 1926.

Feeling responsible for having led the Hashemites into Lloyd George's political wilderness, the much-decorated Colonel Lawrence sought his own wilderness in 1922 by joining the RAF, as AC2 John Ross, the lowest possible rank. He used a false age but gave Tremadog as his place of birth. Only two months later he transferred to the Tank Corps as Pte.Thomas Shaw, with another false birthday, but again retaining his correct Welsh birthplace. Not admitting to any formal education, let alone his Oxford degree, he was sent on a course to obtain a lowly third class certificate of Army Education. In 1925 he returned to the RAF as AC2 Thomas Shaw.

In 1930 St Andrew's University offered T.E. Lawrence an honorary doctorate. He rejected it after pondering, in a letter to a friend, which would sound the more incongruous Dr Aircraftman Shaw or Aircraftman Dr Shaw. He was discharged in March 1935 to become Mr Edward Smith. His real name was preserved with pride for many years in the books of Davies Bryan & Co., where senior salesman Robert Hughes sold him some new shirts upon his return from the Arabian desert. Alas, no one ever asked him why he had gone to such pains to proclaim his Welshness.

Lloyd George's New Jerusalem

The following is the text of a lecture given by the author to the Friends of the Lloyd George Museum, at Llanystumdwy, in May 1999.

'To make the assurance of his fame doubly sure, Mr Lloyd George has indissolubly linked his name with the story of the Eternal People, and thus he becomes a sharer of Israel's immortality.' The words are those of Dr Joseph Hertz, Chief Rabbi of the British Empire, speaking at University College, London, in May 1925.

Lloyd George remains one of the great heroes of Israel. There is a modest street named after him in Jerusalem, complete with trilingual (Hebrew, Arabic and English) nameplates at either end. There is another Lloyd George Street in Tel Aviv. They have survived all the renaming of streets that took place after the British left in 1948. More significantly, there is a whole kibbutz named after him in the Galilean highlands, on the ridge between Tiberias and Haifa. It is called Ramat David, meaning David's Heights, but in post-1948 Israel is now given the politically correct Hebrew pronunciation Ramat Daweed. It was first settled by Jews in 1930, having been chosen as a more defensible site than two earlier kibbutzim, Ayanot and Hasharon, which combined their resources.

Their archives reveal many long arguments about the proposal to adopt the name of a Welsh gentile, albeit one with a Jewish first name. The main argument in favour was his role in fathering the Balfour Declaration. In turn the kibbutz gave its name to RAF Ramat David, a fighter base built beside the settlement in 1942, and now an important facility for the Israeli air force – the world's only military base named after David Lloyd George.

Soon after the kibbutz was established Lloyd George was asked to supply a photograph of himself, and this was duly framed and hung in the dining hall, where I first saw it in 1947 – while searching for any terrorist weapons that might be hidden away for the murder of British troops. It was still hanging in 1954 when Lady Megan Lloyd George read something I had written about it in the *Caernarvon & Denbigh Herald.* She came into the old Herald Office, in Castle Square, Caernarfon, to say: 'I have never heard of Ramat David: tell me more' – and within a few months she had taken herself off to the new Israel, to see the place for herself. Her visit is still cherished in the kibbutz, but by today her father's framed photograph is kept in the archives, from where it was brought out and displayed in 1988, when the Maelgwn choir, based on the Llandudno area, and soloist Mary Lloyd Davies, gave a memorable concert in the new dining hall.

All this seems very jolly and fraternal, but did Lloyd George really deserve the adulation of the Jews, or was he never more than the wiliest of opportunist politicians, ever ready to seize the moment with an appropriate speech? More significant than Ramat David or Lloyd George Street is a letter in the Herzl Museum, Jerusalem, initialled by Lloyd George on the notepaper of Lloyd George, Roberts & Co, solicitors, of 63 Queen Victoria Street, London EC. Dated 1 July, 1903, and addressed to Leopold J. Greenberg, of Fordwych Road, London. With the cross-heading 'Settlement in British East Africa,' the letter said: 'We now beg to send you fair copy of the draft terms and conditions on the concession herein, together with a carbon copy which we thought you might perhaps care to have by you. Will you kindly acknowledge receipt'.

Without the cross-heading it would not have told us very much. Greenberg was a London journalist and well-known Zionist, who had arranged for Austrian journalist Theodor Herzl to come to Britain, to address the 1902 Royal Commission investigating the problems of cheap labour, arising out of the arrival in London of huge numbers of Russian refugee Jews. Herzl told the Commission: 'If you find they are not wanted here, then some place must be found to which they can migrate without raising the problems that confront them here. These problems will not arise if a home be found for them which will be legally recognised as Jewish'.

Ottoman-owned but British-administered Cyprus appealed to Herzl, but it was realised the Turks would never agree. Herzl was more optimistic in suggesting El Arish, then a small but ancient coastal town 90 miles east of the Suez Canal, in Egypt's Sinai desert – nearer

The Bryan family's long association with Caernarfon began in about 1880
when John Davies Bryan was appointed manager of Yr Afr Aur, the famous
drapery stores of Pierce & Williams, in Turf Square. At that time the firm
occupied two shops, on opposite corners of Eastgate Street, as shown in this
photograph – with a golden goat cantilevered from the corner of the building
on the left. When Lloyds Bank acquired the shop on the right Yr Afr Aur took
over the shop of E. Owen in the left foreground of this picture. After World
War II the golden goat was given a new home in a shop window in Pwllheli.

John Davies Bryan, founder of the Egyptian business, whose name still appears on modern maps of Cairo.

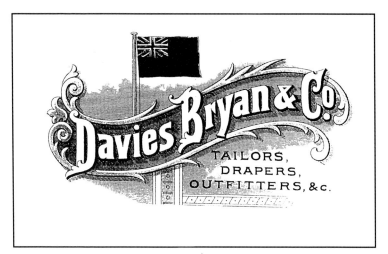

Note heading of Davies Bryan & Co.

John Davies Bryan's first Cairo store, in the ground floor of the Grand Continental Hotel – where Lord Carnarvon spent his winters.

An early photograph of the shop in which John Davies Bryan set up the first fixed-price drapery business in Cairo – and which was later to be taken over by Fred Purslow, of Wrexham.

The 1st Battalion of the Welch Regiment marching through Old Cairo in 1888

The ancient remains of Al Fustat, the original Arab Cairo, whose inhabitants devised the fustian weave much favoured for the strong trousers – trwsus Ffestin – worn by the slate quarrymen of North Wales.

The Alexandria shop specially built for Davies Bryan & Co.

An early photograph of the Alexandria shop of Davies Bryan & Co.

Lawrence of Arabia (T.E.Lawrence), painted in 1919 by Augustus John.

*Sarah Junner, mother of T.E.Lawrence,
photographed in 1910.*

*Gorphwysfa, Tremadog, the house in which
T.E.Lawrence was born.*

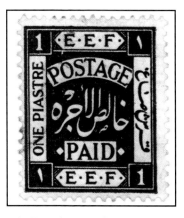

An Egyptian Expeditionary Force postage stamp issued to soldiers of the 53rd Welsh Division in 1916.

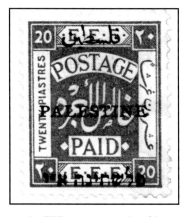

An EEF stamp overprinted in Arabic, English and Hebrew for the invasion of Palestine in 1917.

The introductory title frame for the film which David Lloyd George suppressed on the eve of its intended first showing at Cardiff in 1918, after the magazine John Bull revealed it had been made by a company of covert German Jews using new English names.

Today,s view of the gable end of the Music for All hall which, after being opened as a cultural venue for servicemen, figured prominently in the life of the British garrison in World War II Cairo.

Now a hive of small workshops, the front rooms of Music for All, in Cairo's Maruf Street, once housed debating, music and card rooms, and a restaurant run as a branch of the city's famous Groppis. It was in one of these rooms that future Welsh MP Leo Abse found his political teeth – for which he was expelled to Britain.

A 1996 view of the hall in which the Cairo Eisteddfodau of 1943 and 1944 were held. The Arabic slogan suspended from the roof space, of what is now a garage, says: 'In the name of Allah the Merciful, the Compassionate, and Him we ask for aid.'

Title page of the first issue of Seren y Dwyrain, published in October 1943 for Welsh servicemen in the Middle East, and whose traditions are now perpetuated in Yr Enfys, the journal of Wales International formed by the veterans of the Cairo Eisteddfod.

The throne of the Bishop of Cairo, an Anglican See founded by the Right Reverend Llewellyn Gwynne, of Swansea, who presided over the 1943 Cairo Eisteddfod. The device resembling the Red Dragon, in the coat of arms devised for the first bishop, is actually the winged lion of St. Mark, but was believed to have been painted in red as a tribute to Bishop Gwynne's Welsh roots.

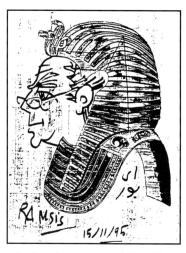

The new Cairo Cathedral whose design was inspired by the lotus flower which figures in countless ancient Egyptian carvings.

An Egyptian cartoon of the author, Ivor Wynne Jones.

Ivor Wynne Jones amidst the debris of war in the sands of Egypt.

More than 3,000 years old, the mortuary temple harpists of Ramses III, copied at Medinet Habu by Emile Prisse d'Avennes.

The Sphinx and pyramids of Giza.

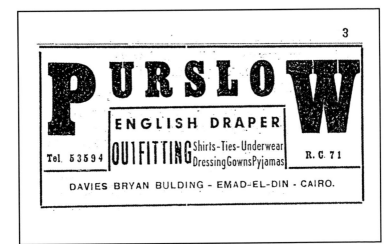

A World War II advertisement of Fred Purslow, the last Welsh owner of the Davies Bryan store.

to the Palestine he said was his ultimate goal. Just a few inches away from the Lloyd George letter, in the Herzl Museum, one can see an exhibit labelled: 'Compass of Colonel A.E. Goldsmid (1846-1904), a member of the Expedition'. That is a reference to the 1903 exploration of a possible site for Herzl's Israel, in Egyptian Sinai. One can just about read the name of Colonel Albert Edward Goldsmid on a very weatherworn 1896 commemorative stone, to the left of the entrance of the former Cardiff New Synagogue, in Cathedral Road, which was converted into offices in 1992. When I photographed it a quarter of a century ago, the inscription still reminded us that Goldsmid was commandant of the 41st (Welsh) Regimental District, at Maindy Barracks, Cardiff.

What a strange Welsh Zionist hotchpotch we have here! In the early 1890s Goldsmid had worked actively for a Belgian millionaire's plan to resettle the persecuted Jews of Eastern Europe in Patagonia, as neighbours of the Welsh. He became the first supervisor of the scheme and arrived at the first Argentine Jewish settlement in a carriage drawn by four white horses, and wearing the colourful full-dress uniform of a Lieutenant-Colonel.

A meeting with that same Belgian millionaire prompted Theodor Herzl to write his *Der Judenstaat*, subtitled 'An attempt at a modern solution to the Jewish question'. It was published in Vienna in February 1896, and formed the basis for the world's first Zionist Congress, at Basel, Switzerland, in 1897. Out of that Congress grew a proposal to find a new

Jewish homeland, and to that end Goldsmid joined engineer Leopold Kessler's exploratory expedition to El Arish in 1903. The town had been fortified by the Pharaohs, rebuilt by the Ottomans in 1536, and restored by Napoleon in 1799 (and was destined to be destroyed by British artillery in 1917).

However, the Sinai scheme collapsed in May 1903, when it was rejected by the Egyptian Government, in a letter signed by Foreign Minister (and future Prime Minister) Butrus Ghali. In that same month, Joseph Chamberlain, Colonial Secretary in Arthur Balfour's Conservative Government, came to the rescue with the offer, to journalist Greenberg, of land for a new Jewish State in what he mistakenly called Uganda – Chamberlain's promised land was actually part of Kenya.

Herzl brought Lloyd George into the picture, at a time when he was just the Liberal MP for Caernarfon Boroughs, and when the Conservatives were in Government. But the London office of his legal practice was earning fame in political circles and that was where the charter for the proposed new Eretz Israel in East Africa was drafted – within just six weeks.

What had attracted Theodor Herzl, father of modern Zionism, to Welsh solicitor David Lloyd George? At that time anyone who cared to dig deeply enough would have judged Lloyd George the politician to be distinctly anti-Semitic. Speaking about the Boer War, at Carmarthen, in 1899, he said: 'The people we are fighting for, those Uitlanders, are German Jews – 15,000 to 20,000 of them. Pah! fighting for men of that type'.

Perhaps the eccentric Colonel Goldsmid, from Cardiff, was the common factor between Herzl's dream and Lloyd George's opportunism. At any rate the Welsh MP became a powerful supporter of the abortive Uganda Plan during the resultant 1904 Parliamentary debate. During that phase Lloyd George would almost certainly have come into contact with Chaim Weizmann, a Russian refugee working as a research lecturer in biochemistry at Manchester University. Weizmann had espoused Zionism at the second Zionist Congress (also at Basel) in 1898 – when he could, of course, never have envisaged his becoming the first president of Israel just half-a-century later.

Herzl submitted his Uganda Plan and Lloyd George's charter to the sixth Zionist Congress, on 23 August, 1903, saying: 'Zion this certainly is not, and can never become. It is no more than aid for the Jews through settlement, but, be it noted, on a national and state foundation'. Not Eretz Israel but ersatz Israel, an autonomous Kenyan-based British colony that would provide a national home for the internationally persecuted of the Diaspora. But the Congress was sharply divided, and although it voted to send an investigative commission to East Africa (with 295 voting for the commission, 177 against, and 100 abstaining) the Zionist movement was split so acrimoniously that the Uganda Plan was never likely to be accepted. Furthermore it was by then opposed by the British colonists in East Africa, and the resultant upheaval was blamed for Herzl's fatal heart attack in July 1904, aged only 44.

Presumably Lloyd George's brief solicitor's liaison with his Zionist clients would normally have ended there, but politics was soon to take over. In 1916 Lloyd George found himself serving as Minister of Munitions, in the worst war the world had even seen. In the midst of the slaughter in the trenches Lloyd George was advised that he was in very real danger of not being able to keep the guns supplied with cordite, because of the shortage of wood alcohol, otherwise called acetone. 'One day the family was joined at breakfast at 11 Downing Street by C.P. Scott, editor of the *Manchester Guardian*,' Lady Olwen Carey Evans told me, in 1989. 'My father asked Mr Scott to find him a scientist who could make acetone. When Mr Scott asked how much time was allowed my father told him he wanted an immediate response – and within a short time Dr Chaim Weizmann had produced his synthetic acetone,' recalled Lady Olwen.

It was in March 1916 that Weizmann was approached by Sir Frederick Nathan, head of the Admiralty powder department, who explained the serious shortage. Weizmann abandoned his academic life to take on the challenge, working four days a week in Manchester and the remaining three in London. After many months of disappointment he was able to start production in a gin distillery at Bromley, and Lloyd George's political career was not only saved but quickly enhanced.

Moving into 10 Downing Street in December 1916, Lloyd George was succeeded as Minister of Munitions by Edwin Montagu, a Jew, who resigned before the end of the month. That prompted the new Prime Minister to say, contemptuously: 'He sought cover, as was the manner of his race; grew hollow-cheeked under the strain'. Hardly the words of a devoted friend of the Jews!

Lady Olwen also recalled being present at 10 Downing Street when Lloyd George offered Weizmann an honour for his invention. 'Dr Weizmann said the only reward he wanted was a national home for Jews, in the Palestine we were then taking from the Turks, hence the declaration of British intent signed by Foreign Secretary Balfour,' she added.

It was an opportune moment for everyone. The grateful former Minister of Munitions was now the ambitious coalition Prime Minister who, as a distraction from the military disasters in France and Flanders, turned his attention to Cairo and constant reminders that the 53rd Welsh Division had crossed the Suez Canal into Sinai. He dismissed the defeatist General Murray, commanding the Egyptian Expeditionary Force, in June 1917, and despatched General Allenby to Cairo to take his place, with orders to capture Jerusalem 'as a Christmas present for the British nation'.

With the 53rd Welsh Division, made up of pre-war Territorial Army volunteers, in the forefront of Allenby's EEF campaign, it soon became apparent that they would indeed deliver Jerusalem by Christmas. Despite the telegrams of death arriving daily in Wales, there was general jubilation at the news of Welsh successes at places with such familiar Biblical names as

Jericho, Bethlehem and Bethany. Emotions were running high, and everything Lloyd George had heard about Palestine, via his fundamentalist Bible-based Christianity of the Scotch Baptists at Cricieth, must have come flooding back to him.

On 2 November, 1917, Foreign Secretary Balfour sent his famous letter to Lord Rothschild, and it was immediately elevated to something called the Balfour Declaration, as though it were a new-found Mosaic tablet from Sinai. It might have been more honestly described as Lloyd George's 'thank you' letter to Chaim Weizmann. 'I have much pleasure in conveying to you, on behalf of His Majesty's Government, the following declaration of sympathy with Jewish Zionist aspirations which has been submitted to, and approved by, the Cabinet,' began the brief letter.

'His Majesty's Government view with favour the establishment in Palestine of a national home for the Jewish people, and will use their best endeavours to facilitate the achievement of this object,' it continued – and that is where it would appear to conclude, if one relied upon the quotations of Zionist apologists for the subsequent fate of the Palestinian Arabs.

In fairness to Lloyd George and to Leopold Amery, the assistant secretary to the War Cabinet, who actually composed the so-called Balfour Declaration, the letter continued: 'it being clearly understood that nothing shall be done which may prejudice the civil and religious rights of existing non-Jewish communities in Palestine, or the rights and political status enjoyed by Jews in any other country'. The letter concluded: 'I should be grateful if you would bring this declaration to the knowledge of the Zionist Federation'.

Conservative MP Leopold Amery was actually a secret Jew, who went to a lot of trouble to conceal his background, even in his 1953 autobiography. His middle name is always quoted as Maurice. It was actually Moritz, which began in Hungary two generations earlier as Moses. Lloyd George had no cause to know Amery's secret, and we do not know what effect such knowledge might have had, when the War Cabinet looked at Amery's Declaration, which was adopted with only two minor changes, and formally signed by Balfour. Amery's son John was hanged for treason in December 1945, having spent three years of the war broadcasting for the Nazis from Berlin. The studio, in the old Olympic Stadium offices, was shared with Haj Amin al Husseini, the Grand Mufti of Jerusalem, and leader of the 1936 Arab Revolt against the Balfour Declaration.

Only a month after the War Cabinet's Balfour Declaration, Turkish troops surrendered Jerusalem to Allenby, and the Welch Regiment mounted the first Christian guard at the Jaffa gate since the medieval Crusades. They did it in time for Christmas, as Lloyd George had demanded.

'Acetone converted me to Zionism,' said Lloyd George, in May 1925, at a meeting of the Jewish Historical Society of England (established in 1893). 'I owe a deep debt of gratitude to Dr Weizmann, and I am his proselyte. In the Ministry of Munitions I was confronted with one of the most serious crises with which I was ever beset. It was one of those unexpected things that come upon you like a cavalry charge coming up against a chasm. And I found such a chasm. As I marched from gun to gun, from shell to shell, I suddenly found that we had not got one of the great motive powers to make cordite – wood alcohol. I turned to Dr Weizmann, and we were saved.

'I felt a deep debt of gratitude, and so did all the Allies, to the brilliant scientific genius of Dr Weizmann. When we talked to him and asked him: "What can we do for you in the way of any honour?" he replied: *"All I care for is an opportunity to do something for my people."* It was worth anything to us in honour or in coin of the realm, but all he asked for was to be allowed to present his case for the restoration of his people to the old country that they had made famous throughout the world. So the case was put before us, and when the War Cabinet began to consider the case for the Declaration, it was quite unanimous in favour. I think we secured the co-operation of the French at that time, and the famous Balfour Declaration was made. There is no man with a greater part in the conversion of the Gentiles running the war than my friend Dr Weizmann,' added Lloyd George.

Note the caveat about Lloyd George's *thinking* he had obtained French support! The French, always a selfishly unreliable ally, had their own very distinctive agenda for the Levant and saw no good in a scheme which would strengthen the British position as self-appointed permanent protector of Zion reborn, in the fertile Mediterranean heartland of what the Arabs always regarded as Greater Syria – the land which Lawrence of Tremadog naively thought he was securing for the Hashemites.

Lloyd George's ambivalence to the Jews has been suggested more recently by a team of impressive researchers restoring the suppressed film of *The Life Story of David Lloyd George*, made during 1918. It was withdrawn before its intended first showing at Cardiff, in November, following an article by Horatio Bottomley in *John Bull*. Under the subheading of 'Britain for the British' Bottomley referred to 'the gallant little Welshman' and said: 'Take the much-advertised film of the life of the Prime Minister. It is being produced by the Ideal Film Renting Company. But what is the composition of the company? I have before me the latest Return filed with the Joint Stock Registry, and this is how the Board is described:

NAME	FORMER NAME	OCCUPATION
Harry Rowson	Harry Rosenbaum	director
Simon Rowson	Simon Rosenbaum	statistician
Sara Wilmot	Sara Wöhlgemuth	widow
Simon Gilbert	Simon Gelberg	journalist
A.M. Kay	A.M. Keppel	secretary

'It is only right to say they all declare themselves to be British,' said Bottomley, who then proceeded to list the shareholders, all with obviously German Jewish names. 'By some blood affinity they were all drawn together into a trade organisation in competition with firms of a truer all-British ring,' he said.

It is not clear whether Bottomley's racism was directed against 'gallant little Welshmen,' Germans or Jews, or all three, but there were plenty of anti-Semites in England ready to feed on his prejudices. The view of those who have now rescued the suppressed film is interesting. David Berry, of the Wales Film & Television Archive, suggests Lloyd George initially agreed to the film with little idea of who ran the company 'and was only apprised when *John Bull* printed a list of executives and shareholders, and the names suggested the Jewish roots of all the company's principals.

'It seems probable that Lloyd George was far less worried by Bottomley's "Hun" rantings than the more realistic vote-losing possibilities, on the election eve, of making a film for a Jewish concern in such xenophobic and racist times,' suggests Berry. 'The danger to his career from this ethnic association might have been uppermost in his mind, whatever his personal views on the Jews in 1918,' adds Berry. At any rate Lloyd George was scared off, and the film was never released.

My view is that Lloyd George does not deserve the reputation he enjoys in modern Israel. Before anyone tells me to read *Is It Peace?* I had better say I am fully familiar with it. The chapter derived from a speech made by Lloyd George in July 1923 might be quoted as his own eloquent defence, but I read it as sugary political cant, by the Welsh Gentile anointed with Jewish acetone. However, let me give you the flavour of the opening paragraph: 'Of all the bigotries that savage the human temper there is none so stupid as the anti-Semitic. It has no basis in reason; it is not rooted in faith; it aspires to no ideal; it is just one of those dank and unwholesome weeds that grow in the morass of racial hatred. How utterly devoid of reason it is may be gathered from the fact that it is almost entirely confined to nations who worship Jewish prophets and apostles, revere the national literature of the Hebrews as the only inspired message delivered by the Deity to mankind, and whose only hope of salvation rests in the precepts and promises of the great teachers of Judah,' etc, etc.

Reviewing the restoration of the Jews to the Palestine from which the Romans had dispersed them two millennia earlier, Lloyd George continued: 'Jewish settlement started with Sir Moses Montefiore's experiment in 1854 – another war year. The Sultan [of Turkey] had good reasons for propitiating the Jews in that year, as the Allies had in 1917'. So there we have it, once again. It was a political expediency of war to make promises to Jews in 1917.

In giving evidence to the Palestine Royal Commission, in 1937, Lloyd George said his Balfour Declaration was made 'due to propagandist reasons'. The Commission was appointed to look at the problem of the 1936 Arab revolt against the Zionist mass migration, into a Palestine from which they had been expelled in AD 73. When presiding over his 1917 War Cabinet, to promote his grateful promise to Chaim Weizmann with the Balfour Declaration, Lloyd George could never have envisaged the rise of Adolf Hitler a mere 16 years later, and the racist purge which caused the Jews of Europe to seek refuge in a British Palestine which Semitic Arabs had populated for two-thousand years.

The Palestine Royal Commission asked Lloyd George to describe how the Balfour Declaration came about. 'He outlined the serious position in which the Allied and Associated Powers then were,' reported the Commission. 'The Roumanians had been crushed. The Russian army was demoralised. The French army was unable at that moment to take the offensive on a large scale. The Italians had sustained a great defeat at Caporetto. Millions of tons of British shipping had been sunk by German submarines. No American divisions were yet available for the trenches.

'In this critical situation,' (Lloyd George told the Commission), 'it was believed that Jewish sympathy or the reverse could make a substantial difference one way or the other to the Allied cause. In particular Jewish sympathy would confirm the support of American Jewry, and would make it more difficult for Germany to reduce her military commitments and improve her economic position on the Eastern Front. Those were the circumstances in which the British Government issued the Balfour Declaration'.

That was the evidence of Lloyd George at a time when Palestine was in the midst of a civil war between Semitic cousins of opposing religions, as the indigenous Semitic Arabs saw what British colonialism and Zionist zeal was doing to their fatherland. How ironic that the Arabs had supported Tremadog-born Lawrence of Arabia's campaign, at the behest of the very same War Cabinet, led by Lloyd George, to liberate Greater Syria from the Turks. The Al Aksa Mosque, in Jerusalem, still stands shoulder to shoulder with the shrines of Mecca and Medina, as one of the Three Holy Mosques of Islam. Unfortunately it stands on the site of Solomon's Temple, beside the Arab Dome of the Rock, the readily recognisable cliché symbol of Jerusalem.

There, I am afraid, is David Lloyd George's selfish political chicanery on which the State of Israel has been built. As for *Is It Peace?* in Lloyd George's New Jerusalem, we all know the answer to that!

Cairo's Welsh Bishop

One of the first customers at the Khartoum shop of Davies Bryan & Co. was Llewellyn Henry Gwynne, of Swansea, who was destined to become the first Bishop of Cairo and play a leading role in the Cairo Eisteddfod of 1943. He was born, at Cilfai, in 1863, one of several children of schoolteachers Richard and Charlotte Gwynne. From Swansea Grammar School three of the brothers went on to become priests of the Church of England. Llewellyn was ordained in 1886, his first appointment being curate at St Chad's, Derby. Three years later he moved to a curacy at St Andrews, Nottingham, from where he became vicar of the neighbouring parish of Emmanuel in 1892. All the time he wanted to be a missionary overseas, and in 1899 the

Church Missionary Society sent him to the newly re-conquered Sudan, on a salary of £12-10s (£12.50) a month.

He was delayed for several days in Cairo, because of mopping up operations in the wake of the 1898 war, and it was during this period that he made the acquaintance of Edward Bryan, in a city where he was dismayed by the stark juxtaposition of great wealth and appalling poverty. On 24 November the Khalifa of Sudan was ambushed, and killed, and Gwynne was allowed to proceed south. He had been given vivid descriptions of the journey by his journalist brother Howell, who had accompanied General Horatio Kitchener on both of his expeditions culminating in the Battle of Omdurman. It was to a congregation of soldiers in the harem of the former Khalifa's palace, in Omdurman, that he conducted the first Church of England service in Sudan.

Gwynne was consistently prohibited from doing any missionary work in northern Sudan, first by General Kitchener and then by General Wingate, so as to prevent his giving credibility to the Egyptian claim that Britain had seized the country only for the purpose of converting the Muslims to Christianity. In 1902, however, Lord Cromer, consul-general in Egypt, granted permission for Gwynne to establish a CMS school in Khartoum. A foundation stone for a planned Khartoum cathedral was laid in 1904 (by Queen Victoria's daughter Princess Henry of Battenburg) but nothing much else happened for some years. In 1905 Gwynne was appointed Archdeacon of Sudan, and in

1907 became the first Suffragan Bishop of Khartoum, which was then part of the diocese of Jerusalem. The next logical step was to point out that the new bishop needed a cathedral, and an appeal was launched, using the emotive public relations tag of saying it was for a memorial to former governor-general General Charles Gordon, who was killed in the Mahdist attack on the town in 1885. The cathedral was consecrated in 1912.

Bishop Gwynne was home on leave when World War I broke out. Instead of returning to Sudan he volunteered for the Royal Army Chaplain's Department, and sailed to France as a captain. Less than a year later he was called back to the War Office, in London, and appointed Deputy Chaplain-General, with the august rank of major-general.

It was the summer of 1919 before he was able to return to Khartoum, where he was touched to be greeted by the Sudanese Police band playing *Men of Harlech*, in recognition of his national roots. In 1920 the diocese of Jerusalem was divided, and Gwynne became the first bishop of the new diocese of Egypt & Sudan, for which the little church of St Mary, in Shari Doubreh, Cairo, became the pro-cathedral. There was also All Saints church, regarded by Anglicans as the original 'parish church' of what was effectively colonial Cairo. Having established a cathedral in Khartoum, Gwynne found himself with the problem of establishing a proper episcopal throne in Cairo, for which Adrian Gilbert Scott was engaged as architect. Initially the Anglican community expressed their worries about the potential running costs of the planned building but eventually enthusiasm prevailed. All Saints church was sold for demolition and redevelopment in a growing commercial area, and St Mary's was sold to another denomination. The money provided the nucleus of a building fund for what was to be called All Saints Cathedral, on a choice site overlooking the Nile, near the Egyptian Museum. Archbishop William Temple, of York (later Archbishop of Canterbury) consecrated the new cathedral in 1938.

Bishop Gwynne had little time for the newly-crowned King Faruk, and the two men fell out when Gwynne refused to sign the visitors' book at the Abdin Palace, making it known he objected to the king's lifestyle. However, when the king gave a dinner for Archbishop Temple, after the consecration service, Bishop Gwynne found himself sitting next to Faruk, who said he would like to visit the cathedral. A tea party was arranged at Bishop's House after which the king commented on the poor quality of the wooden grills on either side of the high altar. Gwynne said the congregation had worked within their means and someday hoped to replace such embellishments. Faruk promptly offered to provide replacement bronze grills, and these were soon made and installed.

As with World War I, Bishop Gwynne was home on leave when World War II broke out. By then 75 years old, he tendered his resignation to the Archbishop of Canterbury – who refused to accept it. This time he returned to his diocese, on a voyage that lasted a month because of diverting far into the Atlantic to avoid enemy submarines. The war injected new life into Cairo cathedral, including the services of an RAF corporal, Clifford Harker, as organist and choirmaster. Welsh servicemen quickly homed in on the Welsh bishop, and were prominent in a new cathedral choral society of 70 members that gave several memorable concerts to packed congregations. These included two performances of the *Messiah* a few days before the famous Battle of El Alamein, some 180 miles to the north. Gwynne would also travel out of Cairo to hold services for the troops in the front line. 'After the service was over,' he once recorded in a letter, 'a young soldier turned up, who had managed to make his way for some 20 miles. He was from my own village in South Wales and had been told by his father, who was a Methodist minister, that he must make every effort to meet with me if he knew where I was to be found'.

Having been the first bishop suffragan for the Sudan, and then the first Bishop of Egypt & Sudan, he was to become the first Bishop of Cairo, when his diocese was divided while he was packing ready to retire in 1946. With his seat in Cairo, his full title was Bishop of Egypt with North Africa, Ethiopia and Somalia. Armorial bearings were needed for the new See, and a Welshman could be excused for believing it to incorporate the Red Dragon – something which may well have been in the designer's mind when using red for the somewhat similar winged lion of St Mark, between two Jerusalem crosses, above a pyramid on a background of heraldic water symbolising the Nile, the Mediterranean and the Red Sea.

Disappointed that Rommel's *Afrika Korps* had failed

to liberate them from Britain's 1882 invasion, post World War II Egyptian nationalists stirred up widespread unrest within weeks of the war's ending. Bishop Gwynne had just finished lunch one day in February 1946 when two of his women staff came to report they had just removed burning petrol-soaked rags that had been piled up against the cathedral door. The bishop went into the cathedral to find stones being hurled through the windows, while Egyptian soldiers stood and watched on the other side of the road. The rioters succeeded in breaking into Cathedral Hall, where they smashed the contents, which they set on fire. While Gwynne was in his office, telephoning the police and fire brigade with appeals for assistance, his house was ransacked and looted of everything symbolising his 47 years of dedicated service on the Nile. The rioters threw his famous English and Arabic oriental library, and most of his papers, into the Nile. It was some two hours later before Egyptian soldiers came out from the adjacent Kasr-el-Nil barracks, to disperse the mob and escort the fire brigade.

Bishop Gwynne returned to Britain particularly distressed at losing his papers and letters that had encapsulated an important phase in the history of Egypt. He made one more visit to Egypt, in 1951, for the dedication of a cathedral window in memory of the men of the 8th Army, who had driven the Germans out of the country following the Battle of El Alamein. Then aged 88, he was invited to join the procession of clergy which, in addition to the Anglicans, included robed bishops and priests of the Coptic, Greek Orthodox,

Armenian Orthodox, Syrian Orthodox, American, French and Egyptian evangelical churches.

The address was given by Field-Marshal Bernard Montgomery, who said: 'We are here today to unveil and dedicate a memorial to the 8th Army, whose name for all time will be linked with this cathedral, with Cairo and the Western Desert . . . I suggest we remember and pay tribute to the friendship between the Church and the fighting man . . . In no place has this friendship been more marked than in this great city of Cairo. Sunday after Sunday in the war years this cathedral was filled to overflowing with British fighting men . . . I was one of them myself'.

He said the window, which incorporated the figure of a youthful Christ holding a model boat in his hands, in the embrace of his mother, represented Christ's going forth from his mother's care to launch a hard, liberating adventure. He asked Bishop Geoffrey Allen to accept the gift of the window. The Bishop of Cairo turned to retired Bishop Gwynne, saying: 'And we request you, our predecessor in this office, who led our diocese during the years of war, to dedicate this window'.

The Right Reverend Llewellyn Gwynne died in December 1957, aged 94. His ashes were laid to rest in the Gwynne Memorial Chapel at Khartoum Cathedral. Adrian Gilbert Scott's fortress-like Cairo cathedral was demolished in 1973-74, to make way for the flyover leading to the new '6th of October Bridge,' which crosses the Nile to Gezira (the Arabic word for 'island'). The name of the bridge commemorates Egypt's surprise crossing of the Suez Canal in 1973, in a tactically brilliant but short-lived victory against Israeli troops that had been well entrenched on the opposite bank since the 1967 War. Egyptian troops were defeated eight days later, but their brief display of newfound military efficiency led to a negotiated Israeli withdrawal from Sinai. It is not without significance that Bishop Gwynne had wanted Jews and Arabs to live in harmony in a united Palestine, and had forecast divisions and animosity across the Middle East in the wake of the 1948 British surrender of its Palestine mandate, and the creation of Israel. He was deeply distressed by the way American, British and United Nations politicians, governed by expediency, had handled the situation in Palestine, and the resultant fate of the indigenous Arabs. He once summed up the situation by declaring: 'Zionism was an egg that the British laid and the Americans hatched; it is bound to be addled'.

The Egyptian government funded the building of the present replacement All Saints Cathedral, on Gezira, at Shari Michel Lutfallah. The foundation stone was laid in July 1977 and the new cathedral was consecrated on St Mark's Day 1988. It was designed by Egyptian architects who have styled the interior like a Bedouin tent. Viewed from the outside, the cathedral is surmounted by a crown inspired by the traditional lotus flower carved on the country's pharaonic temples. The new cathedral preserves the 8th Army memorial window from the original cathedral, in the lady chapel. Other preserved items include the 1938 organ, six marble pillars, a chandelier and the bronze grills given to Bishop Gwynne by King Faruk. These have been reinstalled as wall sections near the entrance. Services are held in English, Arabic, Amharic and Sudanese. The walled compound containing the new cathedral also protects the entrance to a new English Curriculum School, replacing the old British Embassy School.

Lord Carnarvon and Tutankhamun

Perhaps the best-known name in the books of Davies Bryan & Co. was Lord Carnarvon, otherwise George Edward Stanhope Molyneux Herbert, 5th Earl of Carnarvon, who, in 1902 was advised to winter in Egypt because of his health. For his Cairo home he chose the Continental Hotel, cheek by jowl with the city's most famous store. Apart from his long line of descent from the Herberts, and the 18th century gift of his earldom to a son of the 8th Earl of Pembroke, there was nothing at all Welsh about Lord Carnarvon, of Highclere, Newbury. However Welshmen were delighted to embrace anyone with the name of Lord Carnarvon when he was given much of the credit for the discovery, in 1922 of the tomb of Tutankhamun.

Lord Carnarvon was as much of an Egyptologist as he was a Welshman, but he deserves credit for having spent a small fortune on financing 16 years of exploration by Howard Carter, who was dedicated to the discovery of any unknown tomb. The work began in 1907 and it was November 1922 before Carter found the top of a previously unrecorded flight of steps. Unsealing of the tomb was delayed until February 1923, to await the arrival of Lord Carnarvon, and to reveal the most fabulous surviving treasure of the ancient pharaohs.

When revisiting Tutankhamun's tomb in 1996 the author stopped for a drink at the Ramesseum Restaurant of Sheikh Mahmoud abd el-Rasul, the 55-years-old mayor of Gorna, and was surprised to see the walls adorned with photographs of a boy wearing the now-familiar regalia of ancient Egypt's boy king. 'That is my father, Hussein,' explained the mayor. 'As a boy of 12 he used to make the tea for Carter and Lord Carnarvon. When the regalia was discovered Carter let my father wear it before it was all taken to Cairo,' he explained.

Tutankhamun has become the most famous of the Egyptian kings only because his tomb was intact. His funereal gold – enough to wipe out today's Egyptian national debt – was taken to Cairo, but his mummified body still lies in the now open sarcophagus of his tomb, in Thebes.

Sadly, Lord Carnarvon never saw it. A few days after being bitten by a mosquito, while in the Valley of the Kings, he died at the Continental Hotel, on 5 April, 1923, the wound's having become septic. It was 1.55 a.m., and at the precise moment of death the whole of

Cairo was plunged into darkness, while back in England the heir's dog, that had been cared for by Lord Carnarvon, let out a howl and dropped dead. Next day Lord Allenby, the High Commissioner, asked for an explanation for the power failure but the English city engineer had no logical answer. That set in train the legend of the curse of the pharaohs, attributed to an inscription said to have been found on a clay tablet at the entrance, which, when the hieroglyphs were interpreted, proclaimed: 'Death will slay with his wings whoever disturbs the peace of the pharaoh'. Although much quoted, the curse was never photographed, does not appear in the written record of the discoveries, and seems to have disappeared.

Several other unexpected deaths of people associated with the excavation added strength to the legend, and people were quick to point out that Tutankhamun himself had been cursed by a jealous successor who ordered the erasure of his name from all public inscriptions. According to ancient Egyptian philosophy a man's spirit lived on after death for as long as his name was mentioned by the living. In granting immortality to the boy king, Lord Carnarvon had seemingly angered some mysterious Egyptian spirit.

However, the only real evidence of a curse was that of freelance Cairo journalist Arthur Weigall who, after a round of drinks, proposed the toast: 'Let there be a curse on them all for the rest of time'. He was responding to Lord Carnarvon's refusal to give him an account of the discovery because of an exclusive arrangement with *The Times.* Weigall had good cause to feel annoyed for as well as being a journalist he was the Egyptian government's Inspector of Antiquities.

Lady Carnarvon quietly but quickly disposed of everything her husband had brought out of Egypt, so that anyone visiting Highclere would see no trace of the 21 years he had wintered at the Continental Hotel. Other superstitious holders of Egyptian artefacts did the same, in the hope of keeping the curse of the pharaohs at bay. However when the 7th Earl was preparing for opening Highclere to the public, in 1988, an old butler directed him to two secret rooms containing what he called 'the Egyptian stuff'. These priceless items, which had eluded both the 6th earl and his mother, included a death mask of Tutankhamun's father.

The Egyptian government had challenged Lord Carnarvon's claim to ownership of Carter's discoveries, by the time the final chamber of Tutankhamun's tomb was opened on 4 January, 1924, some 3,200 years after being sealed. The Cairo courts ruled in favour of the Government and the entire collection was deposited at the national museum – for which the Egyptian government refunded to Lady Carnarvon the entire cost of her husband's 16 years of sponsorship of Howard Carter.

When Tutankhamun's skull was X-rayed in 1998 Professor Robert Brier, of New York, concluded he had been murdered, dying slowly after a blow from some heavy object. There were fractures at the base of the skull that had started to calcify, showing the 18-years-old king had taken a long time to die. Subsequently he discovered supporting written evidence that he had been assassinated by his elderly chief counsellor Aye who, in the event of the king's death, would inherit his young queen Ankhesenamun, and thus be able to seize the role of pharaoh – a good motive for murder.

Today any Welshman seeing the Tutankhamun room at the Cairo museum basks in some of the reflected glory which still credits Lord Carnarvon with Howard Carter's discoveries.

Bryn Estyn's Egyptologist

We shall never know what fame the forgotten Welsh Egyptologist George Lloyd might have attained, had he not accidentally shot himself at Luxor, on 10 October, 1843. His name does not appear in any written pantheon of Welsh worthies but the Bibliothèque Nationale, in Paris, can tell us he was born in 1815 at Bryn Estyn, Wrexham, a great-grandson of wealthy banking entrepreneur Richard M. Lloyd, of Plas Power, Wrexham.

He was 24 when he joined pioneering French Egyptologist Emile Prisse d'Avennes, also now relatively obscure although both a great scholar and a meticulous draughtsman. Prisse accurately copied countless ancient Egyptian carvings, inscriptions and paintings – including *Bardes de Ramses III, Thebes*, part of which is incorporated in the cover design of this volume.

Prisse was born in 1807 at Avesnes-sur-Helpe, and orphaned in 1814, when he was left in the care of a priest. He trained as an architect and in 1826 briefly joined the Greek insurrection against the occupying Turks. He changed sides and accompanied Muhammad Ali's son Ibrahim Pasha to Alexandria in 1827, joining the French experts who sustained Muhammad Ali's administration.

Initially Prisse was engaged as a water engineer but soon became fascinated by the Orient. He was appointed teacher to Ibrahim Pasha's children and tutor in topography and fortification at the Cairo military institutions – until 1836, when the administration shed most of its Europeans. The unemployed Prisse turned his attention to archaeology, adopted Arab dress and re-named himself Idris Effendi.

At that time the great monuments of Luxor and Karnak were half-buried in centuries of blown sand, in some places up to ceiling level, thus providing convenient rooms that were colonised by the peasants. Many lesser monuments were being robbed to provide building stone for government projects, or tourist souvenirs.

Prisse decided to do something to preserve Egypt's heritage and in 1839 he was joined at Luxor by George Lloyd. The two men made their home in the Karnak temple, also crossing the Nile to live in the tomb of Ahmose (now labelled Tomb No. 83). In addition to his architectural training and artistic skills, Prisse had become expert in reading ancient hieroglyphs, the ancient writing of the pharaohs that had been deciphered only in 1822

We do not know what skills Lloyd was able to contribute to the partnership and neither do we know what took him to Egypt. Their most famous discovery was Egypt's oldest manuscript, now catalogued at the Bibliothèque Nationale, as the *Papyrus Prisse.* Hundreds of drawings and water colours of ancient wall paintings and buildings were ·produced by Prisse. Some of these buildings are now lost and many of the wall paintings are damaged, preserved only in the drawings.

Two events in 1843 brought this valuable work to an abrupt end. Prisse and Lloyd dismantled the List of Kings, in the Hall of the Ancestors, at the Sun-god Amun's temple, Karnak, and smuggled it to Paris, where it is now preserved at the Louvre. The resultant wrath of the Egyptians, and Lloyd's fatal accident, resulted in Prisse's leaving the country in 1844. Back in France he began compiling his first book *Les monuments égyptiens,* containing several of his drawings, which was published in 1847.

Not until 1858 was he allowed to return to Egypt, to continue his pictorial record, but banned from excavation or collection of antiques. He returned to the room in Karnak temple he had shared with Lloyd for four years. Prisse finally left Egypt in 1860, and began work on a magnificently illustrated book with the somewhat long title of *Atlas de l'histoire de l'art égyptien, d'aprés les monuments, depuis les temps les plus reculés jusqu'à la domination romaine* – usually described as the

'Atlas of Egyptian art'. We do not know the extent of Lloyd's input into the drawings. Prisse died in 1879.

Lloyd's Welsh home, Bryn Estyn, was rebuilt during 1903-04 for a Wrexham brewer. It later became an approved school, and subsequently a notorious local authority children's home that became the subject of a Government report in February 2000 into child abuse dating back to 1974.

Music for All

The dormant creativity of Cairo's 123,000 resident servicemen during World War II found a nest in Music for All, the name given by Lady Russell Pasha to the 750-seat former Cinema Odeon, which she reopened for the forces with a piano, a gramophone and her personal record collection. Latent British culture on the Nile blossomed in the autumn of 1943 with such events as the publication of *Oasis: the Middle East Anthology of Poetry from the Forces;* the convening of the first Cairo Eisteddfod, with makeshift Welsh druids; the formation of the short-lived and potentially subversive Music for All Parliament; and the launch of the Welsh-language newspaper *Seren y Dwyrain* (Star of the East).

All were hatched at Music for All, a building which can still be found in a traffic-locked area of Cairo now devoted almost entirely to car repairs. One gable end bears the fading painted inscription Garage Odeon, in an unnamed side street off Shari Maruf, itself a minor street off Shari Suleiman Pasha. Inside is suspended a board running almost from side to side saying (in Arabic): 'In the name of Allah the Merciful, the Compassionate and Him we ask for aid'. Independent workshops now occupy all the original cinema's adjoining shop units in Maruf Street, which Lady Russell had converted into a variety of functional rooms, including a restaurant.

Dorothea Russell was the wife of Sir Thomas Russell Pasha, who had served the Egyptian civil service since 1902, and who was head of the Cairo police from 1917 to 1946, retiring as the last British officer in Egyptian service. Sir Thomas was one of the four lovers of Mirjam Vogt (pronounced Miriam Fukt), wife of the Norwegian Consul General in Cairo, to each of whom she addressed an erotic letter in her book *The Gentle Men*, published in English in 1935, under the pseudonym of Marika Norden. The other three lovers were Cecil Campbell (manager of the Marconi Radio & Telegraph Company, in Cairo), Robin Furness (professor of the English department at Cairo University) and Captain Gordon Waterfield (a journalist on the *Egyptian Gazette* before becoming a wartime commando). It was printed in Paris by the Obelisk Press, chosen by Mirjam Vogt because of the popularity in Cairo of the equally notorious *My Life and Loves*, by Welsh amorist Frank Harris. Three years later Mrs Vogt's book was translated into her native Norwegian and published in Oslo, rapidly becoming a best-seller under the title of *Verdens herrer*, which translates as 'Gentlemen of the world', and which included a fifth letter, addressed to her husband, Stener Heyerdahl Vogt, explaining why she had published the original English edition.

Conscription and Cairo's role as the intelligence and operational HQ for the Mediterranean, the Balkans, and the Arab world, had concentrated a khaki-clad entrepreneurial cross-section of intellectual Britons in the city. Some devoted their energies to the creation of maverick military units like Popski's Private Army, the SAS, an Anglo-Egyptian strand of what became the Forces Broadcasting Service (where Raymond Baxter was to cut his teeth, reading NAAFI News), and the Desert Purchasing Organisation – a mini-Harrods where soldiers could buy gold, silver, ivory, leather and silk souvenirs totally unrelated to the realities of war just a few miles away. The rest found their way to Music for All, where there was an extraordinary burst of activity in September 1943, once the hot Egyptian summer was out of the way, in the wake of the surrender four months earlier of Rommel's *Afrika Korps*.

'Music for All provides a recreation centre primarily for music and talks. It is for all ranks,' said the *Services Guide to Cairo* published in 1943. 'There are four entertainments every night in the air-conditioned Music Room. Four nights a week there are concerts, including a military band; one night a week a gramophone recital (symphonies and operas); one night a talk; and the other night varies from week to week. First class artists only appear, and all the distinguished visiting artists in Egypt can be heard here,' added the Guide. Sunday night concerts by the Cairo Symphony Orchestra, conducted by Squadron Leader Hugo Rignold, became a popular feature, as did visits by ENSA (Entertainments National Service Association). It was during one such ENSA visit that Welsh actor and playwright Emlyn Williams arranged a tea party for Welsh servicemen in the vestry of the Church of Scotland, in Shari Fuad el Auwal

'In addition to this the Centre's own Trio plays from 12 to 1, and from 4.30 to 6.30 pm every day, and there is also something going on every evening from 6 to 6.30, either talks, bridge, chess, or a gramophone recital or concerts. Teas and light refreshments can be obtained in the Music Room during the day. The Restaurant serves fixed luncheons and dinners as well as meals *a la carte,* all served at usual city restaurant prices. The catering is by Groppi.

'The Card Room is open all day and there is also a Sitting Room where poetry-readings, etc, are held. There is a comfortable Reading and Writing Room (air conditioned) where a large selection of papers and periodicals is to be found. There is a ladies dressing room with bath and a woman attendant. The men's bathroom has four baths as well as showers (hot and cold) and a barber's shop. There are two small gardens where refreshments are served. Bridge tables and chess available.

'The entrance fee is PT3 for other ranks and PT5 for officers, and each member of the forces may bring two civilian guests. Civilians with white passes pay PT10 for concerts and lectures. The entrance fee is only PT1 until 2 p.m.,' added the Guide. (PT was the abbreviation for *piastre*, and PT1 was equivalent to 1p of today's UK currency.)

It was in the Sitting Room of Music for All that three soldiers, Denis Saunders in particular, with David Burk and Victor Selwyn (none ranking higher than a corporal) conceived *Oasis*, a book of poetry written by servicemen in the Middle East. After appealing for contributions in the forces programmes transmitted by Egyptian State Radio, and in the pages of the *Egyptian Mail*, they received more than 3,000 poems and were able to print over a hundred in September 1943, under the imprint of the Salamander Society. Keith Bullen, headmaster of the English preparatory school on Gezira, founded the Salamander Society at his home, in 1941, as a meeting place for literary expatriates.

Denis Saunders, alias Almendro the poet, was also a homeopath and osteopath in civilian life. David Burk was a famous pre-war journalist then serving in Cairo as a soldier writing for Political Warfare Executive. Victor Selwyn, an economics graduate, was also a journalist of considerable note. Their anthology was published in an edition of 5,000 copies, and sold for 25 piastres, the equivalent of five shillings Sterling at a time when the average soldier was paid two shillings a day. In his foreword, General Maitland Wilson, Commander-in-Chief Middle East Force, noted that World War II had not been so prolific as the 1914-18 war in the production of poetry, 'perhaps because the tempo is faster and the lands more foreign and barren'. He added: 'I consider *Oasis* very aptly named, because of the pleasure it will give to many who have found war an aesthetic desert'.

In his preface, Dr Worth Howard, Dean of the Faculty of Arts and Sciences at the American University in Cairo, and Director of Literary Activities at Music for All, wrote: 'To the greater portion [of Middle East servicemen] who have found no creative release for their adventures, this anthology should come as a welcome aid.'

'Doubtless,' he said, 'we shall always think of the Battle of Egypt and of North Africa principally in terms of the desert. Airfields have been established and maintained on the sand; men have lived on the desert, enduring its intense hear in summer when a tent might suddenly burst into flames, or its bitter cold in the winter when rains might come to add discomfort and pain. In the swarms of flies and other insects the plagues of ancient Egypt may have seemed revived to require another Moses who never appeared. Men have been lonely; they have been weary; they have been harassed in body and spirit; yet they have been tempered and toughened; they have regained a happy simplicity of living; some have learned the vast resources of the human spirit.'

Turning to Cairo, Dr Worth continued: 'And back they have come from the desert – sometimes bitter, sometimes desperate to catch life in some more colourful aspect – but so often they have returned eager simply for a bath, clean sheets, a good meal. To some it may have appeared that these men back on leave to the city, in their need for change, cared only for the sordid and the ugly

'On the contrary, thousands of men have searched for beauty in a variety of forms. With what evident joy they have flocked to concert halls to hear a Beethoven sonata, a Brahms concerto, a Schubert symphony. Men have crowded the cathedral courtyard to listen to a Handel oratorio. They have sought hungrily for the privilege of good books. Men and officers have gathered to share their love of poetry – others have read and acted plays together. Discussion groups have sprung up, and good speakers on a wide range of topics have been in demand. Let no man say that all those in uniform have become simple cogs in a machine that military discipline has made of them mere automatons. Their eager search for the good and the beautiful has been splendid proof of the cultural vitality of our democratic processes.'

The philosophy of the benevolent British ladies of Cairo, such as Lady Russell, Lady Wavell and Lady Lampson, wife of Ambassador Sir Miles Lampson, was summed up by Brigadier John Ropes, in one of his poems in *Oasis*, part of which read:

We're voluntary ladies serving voluntary beer
To voluntary soldiers compulsorily here . . .

We're voluntary workers selling voluntary eggs
To keep the men's attention from those voluntary legs . . .

We're voluntary ladies in voluntary clubs
Keeping rather browned-off soldiers from the cabarets and
                                                    pubs . . .

As Lawrence Durrell, a sergeant in the Field Security Service, was to say of the 3,000 would-be bardic soldiers who were inspired to put pen to paper for this Music for All exercise, 'the poetic upsurge brought us many eccentrics'. The book quickly sold out, making a profit of £250 which was given to the Red Cross.

The Cairo Eisteddfod

In the eyes of many in the Cairo garrison, the most eccentric event to emerge from Music for All was the Cairo Eisteddfod of 1943, now little more than a mummified memory, quietly fading away into the dust and noise of its unlikely setting. It was convened under the presidency of the Right Reverend Llewellyn Gwynne, Bishop of Cairo.

Welsh troops had become accustomed to assembling at 8 p.m. every Sunday at St John's Methodist Church, which stood across the road from the Church of Scotland in Avenue Fuad el Alwal. As the city's English Methodists departed at the end of their evening service the troops would gather for a Welsh language service, conducted by one of the military chaplains. From time to time a communion service would be held.

These services became famous for their hymn singing, conducted by Flying Officer T. Elwyn Griffiths, a pre-war librarian serving at RAF Heliopolis. He has recalled how, after the evening service, many of the servicemen, who came from a wide variety of units, would make for a nearby café called L'Americain, for a coffee or a tea – and to continue their hymn-singing, in impromptu sessions that attracted a ready audience of Cairenes, some of whom established a pattern of attending regularly to listen to the Welshmen.

Out of that musical tradition grew the Cairo Welsh Society's male voice choir, which used to practice at Wesley House, conducted by the Society chairman, the Reverend E.J. Baker, of Bargoed. Other of the society's meetings were held at the Victory Club, located at the corner of Shari Suleiman Pasha and Shari el-Bustan – which was also the home of the Cairo Cornish Society. The club was founded in 1941 by Brigadier T.F.V. Foster as a centre for troops who wished to meet to discuss and enjoy drama, literature and art. The popularity of the Society's choir, both among the members and other temporary Cairenes who requested concerts, resulted in the creation of the separate Cairo Welsh Glee Party, conducted by Wyatt Day, also of Bargoed, to the piano accompaniment of Leading-Aircraftman Gwyn Bryant, of Hirwaun – with E.J. Baker as chairman and T. Elwyn Griffith first as secretary but later taking over the baton. The Glee Party gave about fifteen concerts, some of which were broadcast by the complicated embryo Forces Broadcasting Service arrangement with Egyptian State Broadcasting (who sought to maintain control over all transmissions on Egyptian soil). Soloists included Stanley Jones (Bangor), Mortimer Lloyd (Brecon), John Evans (Brynsiencyn) and Idwal Jones (Llangoed). Only one woman sang with the Glee

Party. She learnt to sing in Welsh, but her identity has been lost in the sands of time, Elwyn Griffiths believing her to be a Greek called A. Tome, while Handel Morgan, of Rhosneigr, thought she was a Syrian named Tomi.

The enthusiasm of the Cairo Welsh Society hatched the 1943 eisteddfod, which was broadcast to Britain, at a time when it might have seemed bizarre for about 200 uniformed soldiers and airmen, and a few sailors, to assemble in the middle of the war to be asked: *A oes heddwch?* ('Is there peace')? The traditional responding chorus of *Heddwch!* ('Peace!'), repeated thrice, was blended with a few more daring isolated cries of *Salaam!* the Arabic equivalent, which seemed to set the scene into context. Some of the participants had travelled from as far as Iraq, Iran and Cyprus.

Army nurses had been coerced into converting stolen hospital linen sheets into a dozen bardic gowns, but as the only available patterns were a chaplain's surplice, the local *galabiya* and drawings of ancient Egyptian dress in the Cairo Museum, the results were somewhat exotic. Field Hospital Sister M. Davies Jones was the mistress of the robes.

In best Gorsedd tradition, the appointed bards chose pseudonyms linking their specialities to place names, in a mixture of Welsh and Arabic, to create such delightful titles as Pencerdd Misr (i.e. Chief Musician of Egypt), Alaw Suez (Suez Lily), Aethwy'r Aifft (Aethwy from Egypt), Tarw Tura (The Bull of Tura, i.e. Gwilym Robert Davies, of Bala) and Tudur Helio (Tudor from Heliopolis). The 'Archdruid' was Corporal Richard

Aethwy Jones, a Caernarfon bank manager. An eisteddfod choir was recruited under the baton of Elwyn Griffiths. The master of ceremonies was the Reverend E.J. Baker.

A chair thought suitable for the occasion was spotted in the office of a very senior officer at RAF headquarters, from where it was 'borrowed' for the installation of 'Gwyndaf', the pseudonym of Leading-Aircraftman William J. Jones, a Caernarfon bus conductor, as the first chaired bard of the Middle East – who received a miniature oak chair, inscribed 'Cairo 1943' on a silver plaque, to commemorate the event. Predictably, perhaps, the set subject for the poem was *Yr Anialwch* ('The Desert'). The adjudicator was the Reverend Tom Madoc Jones, Chief Other Denominations Chaplain to the RAF in the Middle East. Perhaps W.J. Jones was predestined to win! He was a big man, and long before the war he became generally known in Caernarfon as Will Gaffer, derived from the Egyptian Arabic word *gaffir*, meaning work-gang leader. He even used 'Will Gaff' as his signature on letters to Caernarfon friends posted from Egypt. His success at the Cairo eisteddfod earned him the job of borough librarian in his home town when he returned from the war.

Winners were chosen in all the usual categories, although sadly some of the details are sparse. Dillwyn Miles won the award for a sonnet. He was secretary of the Welsh Society at Jerusalem (where he was to marry in 1944), and was later to become well known as the Grand Sword-bearer for the Gorsedd of Bards (1959-66) at the National Eisteddfod of Wales. The tenor solo contest was won by John Evans, of Brynsiencyn, who subsequently won prizes at several eisteddfodau in Wales. The bass solo winner was Edwin Smith, of Bradford. There was a soprano solo winner: a Sister Bellamy, of Sheffield. The penillion winner was Idwal Jones, of Llangoed, the harp solo winner a T. Jones. The glee party contest was won by an English group: the Royal Engineers' Singers, conducted by William Wolfenden, of Bradford.

In his presidential address the Bishop of Cairo expressed his Welsh pride at witnessing such a successful event, adding that the Welsh were the true Britons and foundation stone of the British Empire. This, the first eisteddfod in Egypt, was, he said, only the second eisteddfod he had ever attended, the other being 66 years earlier when, as a boy of 14 he attended a local eisteddfod at Swansea. 'I still remember the harpists who stirred the Welsh blood,' he said.

Exactly a year later, in September 1944, the second and last Cairo eisteddfod was held in Music for All – under the presidency of a New Zealander, Air Marshal Sir Keith Parke. Many of the Welsh servicemen who had been in Egypt in 1943 had by then been posted to more active theatres of war, in many different parts of the world. The joint secretaries for the second eisteddfod were Handel Morgan, whose home was then in Penrhiwceiber (and who had become chairman of the Cairo Welsh Society), and Islwyn Davies, of Swansea. Upon his return from the war Handel Morgan became a teacher and settled in Anglesey.

The 1944 chair was won by Army chaplain the Reverend D.D. Lloyd Evans, and other prize winners included a Greek and a Mauritian. A winning quartet comprised soldiers from New Zealand, Canada, the United States and Wales, and veterans of this most exotic of eisteddfodau later claimed it to be the true forerunner of the Llangollen International Eisteddfod.

At the instigation of Penrhynside shopkeeper Eric Thomas, formerly of Blaenau Ffestiniog, veterans of the 1943 and 1944 eisteddfodau assembled for the last time at Llandudno's Ebeneser Methodist church hall, during the 1963 National Eisteddfod. Fred Purslow, the last Welsh owner of the Davies Bryan store, was the chairman. It was this writer's privilege to surprise the gathering with a special 20th anniversary message of 'the warmest and sincerest greetings of goodwill' that had been entrusted to him by President Nasser, of Egypt.

Seren y Dwyrain

It was in the Victory Club (now demolished), amid all the preparations for the 1943 eisteddfod, that Sergeant T. Alun Jones, whose home was in South Wales (later a teacher in Old Colwyn), noted there was no Welsh-language news sheet for the area. Elwyn Griffiths took the suggestion on board and was wondering how to maintain the Welsh camaraderie when the first issue of *Air Force News* arrived on his desk. He promptly asked for space for a weekly column of Welsh news but wrote only one such contribution before a change of policy sent him chasing for an alternative – and what better than his own Welsh language newspaper?

He canvassed 25 advance orders from Haifa Welsh Society and another 50 from Alexandria, together with the financial backing of Fred Purslow. Thus equipped, Elwyn Griffiths negotiated a contract with a Cairo printer for 400 copies of a four-page journal which he called *Seren y Dwyrain*, meaning 'Star of the East'. The first issue appeared on 16 October, 1943, a fortnight after the Cairo eisteddfod, edited by himself and Alun Jones. Hand-set in a print shop opposite the then beautiful Ezbekiya Gardens, by a Lebanese compositor totally unfamiliar with the Welsh language, that pioneering issue contained remarkably few errors. His biggest problem was his standard English case of type, with its insufficient supply of the letter 'y' for the Welsh language, requiring him to print it in sections.

Within five months the circulation of *Seren y Dwyrain* had increased to 1,000 copies, across North Africa and east as far as Iraq, and in March 1944 an appeal was launched in Wales for funds that would enable Elwyn Griffiths to extend the distribution to Welshmen throughout Africa and Italy. That, too, was a success and *Seren y Dwyrain* was increased to eight pages, with a circulation of 1,500, eventually rising to 2,000. Out of another appeal by Griffiths, in the pages of his beloved *Seren*, grew a total of seventeen Middle East Welsh societies. With the founder's posting to Italy, the editing of *Y Seren* was taken over by the

Reverend Tom Madoc Jones, and towards the end of the war it was printed by the Army Press in Cairo.

Publication ended in October 1945, when the Reverend Madoc Jones was preparing for demobilisation and return to Llannerch-y-medd. Phoenix-like the journal was immediately reborn in Wales, with the new title of *Yr Enfys* ('The Rainbow'), again edited by Elwyn Griffiths, as the quarterly journal of his new Undeb y Cymry ar Wasgar *(Society of Welsh People in Dispersion)*, which he founded out of the mailing list for the various Middle East Welsh societies he had brought with him from Cairo. The Undeb quickly acquired international popularity, and in 1955 was given a special Friday ceremony at the National Eisteddfod – an event that became an emotional highlight at each annual eisteddfod. It remains one of the festival's outstanding features, as an alphabetical roll call of the nations, during which visiting Welsh residents of those countries stand up to be welcomed by the audience.

Elwyn Griffiths edited *Yr Enfys* until 1988, serving a world-wide society which by then had changed its title to Cymru a'r Byd (Wales International), for which Wales Tourist Board became a partner in the quarterly production of a bilingual quarterly magazine perpetuating the title of *Yr Enfys*.

The introspective Welsh Establishment was unbelievable slow to recognise the work of Elwyn Griffiths, something highlighted by the author on New Year's Day 1989, in his regular column in the *Daily Post*. If merit, logic and justice formed part of the system, wrote the author, someone would have said 'thank you' to Elwyn Griffiths for his 46 years of voluntary work for the Welsh diaspora. Only then did the University of Wales take notice, belatedly giving him an honorary degree in 1990.

However, arising out of his pioneering work in wartime Cairo, Elwyn Griffiths has left a permanent Welsh mark on the Middle East. While planning his 1943 eisteddfod he wrote to the Alexandria, Jerusalem and Haifa Welsh societies, seeking ideas for the welfare of Welsh servicemen. The letter was read to the Haifa Society by secretary Lewis O. Jones, of Blaenau Ffestiniog (later of Rhuthun). RAF Corporal David G. Griffiths (Dei Griff), also of Blaenau Ffestiniog, said he had just visited the Pater Noster Church, on the slopes of the Mount of Olives, overlooking Jerusalem, famous for its display of the *Lord's Prayer* in many different languages – from which it takes its name. The church was founded by Princesse de la Tour d'Auvergne, on a site she had studied from 1857 to 1910, eventually excavating the grotto of the primitive Church of Eleona (the Greek word for olives), built by the Empress Helen (mother of Constantine the Great), who was told in AD 326 that this was the place to which Jesus retreated at night to teach his mysteries and his prayer to his disciples. The founding Princess decreed that her church should belong to all denominations and all languages.

'Dei Griff told us how he was saddened to find there was no Welsh translation at the Pater Noster, and we wrote to Elwyn Griffiths, in Cairo,' Lewis O. Jones told the author. Elwyn Griffiths, who was previously unaware of the Pater Noster church, immediately took up the challenge and enlisted the support of Sir Ifan ab Owen Edwards, founder of Urdd Gobaith Cymru *(Welsh League of Youth)*. He also wrote to Richard Hughes, chairman of Jerusalem Welsh Society, expressing his surprise at the omission of a Welsh translation and inviting Hughes to join in the project, his having emigrated to Jerusalem in 1890, from his native Betws-y-coed. When the Union flag was hoisted over the city in 1918 the new British Mandatory Government enlisted Hughes's knowledge of the Arabs and fluency in Arabic and gave him a job as a land commissioner. His work was to negotiate awkward land deals with the inhabitants, more especially with the Bedouin, who were trying to come to terms with a sudden switch from centuries of Muslim provincial rule to a Christian administration bent upon fostering Jewish immigration.

When Elwyn Griffiths's letter arrived at his home, in Jerusalem's up-market Rehavia district (where Israel's top government ministers now live), Richard Hughes took himself off to the Pater Noster church to use his negotiating skills with the Carmelite nuns. For reasons that have never been explained there was one blank wall space reserved inside the church, despite an overflow into the cloisters and courtyard, displaying the *Lord's Prayer* on mosaic tiles in forty-one languages (82 by today). This choice east-facing wall was offered to Wales, and Sir Ifan authorised Hughes to commission the work, promising that the youth of

Wales would raise the £60 necessary to buy and install the 60 locally-made ceramic tiles on which the Welsh translation is inscribed. The Amen was being cemented into place in 1945 when Emyr Currie-Jones, from Caernarfon, chanced to become the first Welshman to see the completed *Gweddi'r Arglwydd* in place. Later to become a prominent Cardiff solicitor, Currie-Jones was a conscientious objector against military service, working for Save the Children fund, who had posted him to a camp for refugee Greeks at Gaza. For those who know its origins the Welsh display in the Pater Noster church is a memorial of the Cairo Eisteddfod of 1943.

An international celebration was being planned to take place in Cairo in 1998, for the 50th anniversary of the foundation of Undeb y Cymry ar Wasgar. But when 58 tourists were massacred by gunfire, at the west bank temple of Queen Hatshepsut, opposite Luxor, the Council of Wales International announced it had decided 'to exercise caution', declaring it would be unwise to visit Egypt at that time. The few remaining veterans of wartime Cairo, who would have been content to risk the journey, believed the cancellation was due to the cold feet of Welsh Americans, many of whom even cancelled visits to Wales because it was a bit too near to Egypt!

My Life and Loves

Some would claim the most famous of Cairo's Welshmen was Rhiwabon journalist, author and amorist Frank Harris, although he does not appear ever to have visited the city, except in the ubiquity of print. His fame or infamy relied upon the endorsement: MUST NOT BE IMPORTED INTO ENGLAND OR U.S.A. on each of the four paperback volumes of his explicit 889-page autobiography *My Life and Loves.* The importation ban was enough to ensure that thousands of soldiers brought Harris's amorous adventures back to Britain – with Welsh soldiers claiming exemption from the specific ban relating to England and America!

Harris' Welsh pedigree was impeccable – he even claimed descent from Owain Glyndŵr, along with the Harries, Harry and Harhy branches of the ancient family, with whom he shared the warrior prince's 15th century coat of arms and motto. He was born in 1855, the son of Thomas Harris, a steward aboard a Revenue cutter in the Irish Sea, and Anne, the daughter of a Pembrokeshire Baptist minister, the Reverend James Hughes Thomas. The father was born in 1814 at Gilfach Goch, a five-acre smallholding at Fishguard, and began his working life as a Coast Guard, in South Wales. He was on Revenue patrol off Ireland when Frank was born at Galway, and christened James Thomas Harris after his pious grandfather.

The family decided the boy – always known as Frank – should be brought up as a Welshman, and he was sent to Rhiwabon Grammar School, where the Reverend A.L. Taylor was headmaster, under the patronage of Sir Watkin Williams Wynn. He arrived at the beginning of 1868 and it was in August of that year that he discovered the mysteries of sex – something that became a life-long consuming pleasure he was to describe in detail to his Cairo readers.

The awakening occurred while Frank was on holiday in Rhyl, aged 13. He had gone for a late evening walk with 15-years-old Gertrude Hanniford, and they had got almost as far as Abergele when they saw a sudden great glare in the sky, a mile or more away, accompanied by the sound of an explosion. It was the railway collision between the Irish Mail passenger train heading for Holyhead and a runaway quarry explosives train from Llanddulas. The 33 victims lie buried in Abergele churchyard.

Frank and Gertrude made for the scene of the disaster, and that involved climbing over a fence. 'I had thrown myself on the wooden palling and half vaulted, half clambered over it. But Gertrude's skirts prevented her from imitating me. As she stood in dismay a great thought came to me . . . ' he wrote. It was while helping her overcome the incompatibility of layers of long skirts and a high fence, in those knickerless days, that he accidentally discovered Gertrude's hidden anatomy – which he was to describe in some detail.

In the years to follow much more lurid discoveries were to me made and described, in Rhiwabon and the world beyond, and in 1922 Frank Harris published the first volume of *My Life and Loves*, in which he said:

'From 13 to 20 the sex-urge, the lust for flesh was so overwhelming in me that I was conscious only of desire'. It was printed in Germany, but by the time he had completed the 302 pages of the second volume, in 1923, he had turned to a Paris printer – attracting the wrath of the American courts.

Judge Levy, of the New York Supreme Court, said he only had to read a few passages to find it 'disgusting and utterly revolting'. He made an order authorising New York police to enter premises without warrant to seize and destroy the errant Welshman's book. The Obelisk Press, Paris, published all four volumes in 1926, resulting in a ruling by the Nice court that the book 'offended public morals.'

The only accessible market with a big English-reading population was Egypt, where for many years street vendors had been asking soldiers and visitors such questions as: 'You want to see dirty pictures, Johnny?' or 'You want my sister, Johnny?' It was for this market, in the city of King Faruk (discovered in 1952 to be the owner of the world's biggest-known collection of pornography, hidden within the Abdin Palace), that *My Life and Loves* was reprinted in Paris in 1934 (three years after Harris's death), endorsed with the prohibition against importation to England or America. There were further reprints for the lucrative Anglo-Egyptian military market in 1945 and 1948, but within the United Kingdom the book remained 'unfit' for British readers until four years after the groundbreaking *Lady Chatterley's Lover* trial, in 1960.

From puberty Frank Harris became a magnet for the

attentions of women. In her 1969 autobiography, Enid Bagnold (Lady Jones) described her brief affair with Harris in 1912, when she was 22 and he 57, writing: 'Sex, said Frank Harris, is the gateway to life. So I went through the gateway in an upper room at the Café Royal'. In 1920 author Enid Bagnold married Sir Roderick Jones, who was head of Reuter's from 1915 to 1941.

Anyone now reading Frank Harris's *My Life and Loves* will be left wondering what all the fuss was about, but the underlying naiveté of British troops in wartime Cairo made it a sensationally pornographic revelation of a world far removed from Harris's puritanical father, and the Welsh Baptist chapel background of Rhiwabon Grammar School's most notorious pupil.

Soldiers' Parliament

The least known of the Music for All fledglings was the Soldiers' Parliament. It, too, sprang to life in the autumn of 1943, out of one of the hall's discussion groups called Thinking Aloud, held in the Garden Room. British soldiers are normally expected to divorce themselves from political philosophy, and the only approved basis for democratic debate was the Army Bureau of Current Affairs, or ABCA, and its fortnightly discussion notes called *War*, which were endorsed 'Not to be published', with the rider: 'Not to be communicated, either directly or indirectly, to the Press or to any person not holding an official position in His Majesty's Service'.

No military secrets would have been gleaned from these publications. They were a bland basis for patriotic thoughts, which officers were supposed to seed among the men by contrived discussion at compulsory gatherings. For instance, in the issue of 3 April, 1943 there is a feature entitled: 'A chicken saves its bacon', purporting to be extracted from a soldier's letter from Italy's former colony in North Africa. The supposed soldier tells of the amazement of the local Arab 'deputy-mayor' on seeing a chicken roam freely among British troops. With tears in his eyes the 'deputy-mayor' explained to the soldier, seemingly in fluent English: 'Never would a chicken circulate for more than 20 seconds among the local tents'.

The guidance notes for the hapless officer charged with leading the ABCA discussion (often to a group of junior NCOs with much greater intellect), told him: 'Obviously it is important for our troops to produce a similar impression everywhere. Do your men agree with this proposition?'. Alternatively, if dealing with a more aggressive audience, the officer could turn to that week's main feature, entitled: 'Be mean, and kill 'em'.

Conscription had given the Army in Cairo a surplus of intellectual citizen soldiers, who languished unrecognised in the ranks, where they were regarded as second-class citizens specifically banned from places like Shepheard's Hotel, which were reserved for officers. This reservoir of freethinking found an outlet in the Music for All Parliament, with discussions on more lively topics than British mercy for North African chickens.

The 'Parliament' first met on 1 December, 1943. It had been dreamed up by a group of soldiers involved in Army education, as a source of entertainment while stimulating democratic discussion on the kind of Britain that should emerge from the war. It could not have come into being without official encouragement and approval, although no record of such endorsement seems to have survived. In order to ensure compliance with Army regulations it was decided to organise the Parliament into simple 'for' and 'against' groups, with a 'government' and an 'opposition', instead of allowing division on political party lines. The topic for debate was advertised in advance as a 'Bill', such as might be tabled by a post-war Westminster Government, and a 'Speaker' was appointed: a South African barrister serving as a lieutenant.

The opening debate was described as a *Distributive Trades (Nationalisation) Bill.* That pioneer assembly attracted an audience of 150 who passed the 'Bill' with an overwhelming majority. The second debate was on an *Inheritance Restriction Bill*, which was also passed. The debates were drawn to a close after two hours, to encourage the audience not to drift away before the bars closed.

Inevitably, after only two sessions the activities surrounding the 'Parliament' produced a mock election, on 2 February, 1944, when anyone attending Music for All after 8 p.m. could vote. The intention was to try to widen the democratic process beyond a simple left versus right yes/no division. An estimated 400 turned up that night, and as we know from many post-war conversations back in Wales, Welsh soldiers and airmen took a particularly keen interest in the process.

Four 'party' candidates addressed the audience, followed by questions from the floor. About half the audience voted, resulting in an overwhelming victory for Labour, with the Conservative candidate ending up as a very poor also-ran, in fourth place. Private Henry Solomons was appointed 'prime minister' of a new Labour 'cabinet' which would plan future debates. The resultant 'King's speech' was presented to an enthusiastic audience of 500 on St David's Day, when the 'cabinet' proposals included nationalisation of the banks, better pensions, the building of 4m homes in a 10-year plan, an Anglo-Soviet Alliance and an Atlantic Charter – all reported in the *Egyptian Gazette.*

When soldiers and airmen turned up for the next advertised session, on 5 April, they found the word 'parliament' had been cut out of the posters. The session began with Cairo's Army Education Officer, Major Trench, reading an Order from General Stone, Commander of British Troops Egypt, banning the use of the word 'parliament', and the admission of civilians or journalists, and stipulating that all future proceedings would be supervised and controlled by the Education Officer, who would ensure that 'no violent political propaganda and nothing subversive to discipline occurs'. The reason given for the restrictions was that the BBC's Listening Service, at Caversham, had recorded the German radio service's reporting of the 'parliament's' debate (presumably via the *Egyptian Gazette*), with claims that British troops in Cairo were creating Communist Soviets.

The audience immediately objected to the restrictions as incompatible with a war being fought to sustain democracy, the most rousing speech coming from a Cardiff airman named Leo Abse, 'chancellor' in the 'cabinet' – who was to become Labour MP for Pontypool in 1958. This, the sixth, and what turned out to be the last session of the Soldiers' Parliament, closed with a unanimous decision to nationalise the Bank of England.

Alarmed by the April 1944 pro-communist mutiny of the exiled Greek troops based in Egypt, HQ Cairo suddenly saw the Music for All 'parliament' as a subversive British mutiny in the making, and decided to neutralise it. The organisers were ordered to meet on 24 April, to be told of further restrictions – which had been leaked the previous day in the *Egyptian Gazette*. They were to deny admission to allied soldiers, lest they should interpret the activities as mutiny, and were to move the venue, of what would be renamed the Forum, from Music for All to somewhere under direct military supervision, in Kasr el Nil Barracks. Future debates would have to be on Oxford Union lines, with all speeches submitted in advance.

That was the end of the 'parliament', resulting in a debate in the House of Commons on 16 May, 1944 when junior War Minister Edward Grigg said: 'It was certainly known that the Germans had used these meetings for propaganda purposes, suggesting there had been a mutiny. In view of these facts it was decided, in my view quite properly, by the local commander, that the discussions should in future take place under official military control.'

Meanwhile, back in Cairo, arrangements were being made for the immediate posting and scattering of those seen as the trouble-makers – the worst being identified as Aircraftman Leo Abse, who later recalled, in his book *Private Member* (1973): 'That night I nationalised the Bank; but in the morning I was arrested. The military authorities refused my challenge of a court martial and I was taken under escort to Suez, and kept in custody to await the arrival of a boat which was to take me to a hot and arid island in the Persian Gulf, where I was to be quarantined.'

Instead he was posted far away from the Middle East, to the closer observation available at Liverpool, a strategic error that gave him instant access to a more sympathetic left-wing audience. That resulted in more questions in the House of Commons, where Air Minister Sir Archibald Sinclair said: 'When the Army authorities decided to close the Forces Parliament a public protest was organised, in which this airman figured prominently.'

HQ Cairo also rounded on Dr Worth Howard, Honorary Director of Literary Activities at Music for All, for not warning the 'parliament' committee in advance that restrictions were to be announced on 5 April – the surprise which sparked off the resentment and protests. Another victim of HQ's wrath was

Captain Gilbert Hall, a distinguished lecturer serving with the Army Education Corps, who had helped set up the 'parliament'. He was forced to resign his commission and sent home in disgrace. This brief episode came to an abrupt end in the Never-Never land of neutral Cairo at war, but Lady Russell Pasha survived the affair and was awarded the OBE for her work as director of Music for All.

Bryan's X Troop

An inscribed block of Blaenau Ffestiniog slate unveiled at Aberdyfi on 15 May, 1999 could be described as an enigmatic postscript to the saga of the Cairo Cofis. The simple inscription says: 'For the members of 3 Troop 10 (IA) Commando, who were warmly welcomed in Aberdyfi while training for special duties in battle, 1942-43. Twenty were killed in action.' It is an inscription that conceals far more than it commemorates, not least the name of Major Bryan Hilton-Jones, MC, the troop's only commanding officer.

Readers will recall that in the 1929 will of Edward Bryan, of Cairo, there was a bequest for his young grandson Bryan Hilton-Jones – whose first name perpetuated the family's famous surname. Olwen Bryan married Dr Orthin Hilton-Jones, of Harlech, where their son Bryan was born in 1918. Olwen Hilton-Jones inherited the tenancy of Crug, near Caernarfon, but after her divorce spent the rest of her life at

Hendregaerog, South Road, Caernarfon.

After graduating in modern languages, at Cambridge, in 1939, Bryan Hilton-Jones was called up with the first militia conscripts, on the eve of World War II. Initially commissioned into the Royal Artillery, his fluent knowledge of German led to his being siphoned off for intelligence work. On 14 July, 1942 General de Gaulle, head of the Free French government in exile, inspected the French Troop of the new No.10 Inter-Allied Commando, headquartered at Harlech, before sending his men off to Cricieth, while the Dutch Troop was on its way to Porthmadog.

Ten days later X Troop arrived at Harlech. At that stage it comprised only Captain Bryan Hilton-Jones, a Hungarian sergeant and eight privates from Sudetenland, who were later joined at Aberdyfi by another 43 registered aliens, after two months' of intensive interrogation by MI5. As the build-up of the Inter-Allied Commando continued, the Belgians arrived at Abersoch, the Norwegians at Nefyn, and the Poles, first at Fairbourne and later at Caernarfon.

It was Prime Minister Winston Churchill who gave X Troop its mysterious name, declaring: 'They must perforce be considered an unknown quantity. Since the algebraic symbol for the unknown is X, let us call them X Troop.' Some of us think that is the name that should have been inscribed on the Aberdyfi memorial, rather than its innocuous final title of 3 Troop, but the 1999 ceremony was surrounded by unfortunate bickering among survivors who had emigrated to America, a few of whom wanted X Troop to be described as the Jewish

Commando, with accompanying demands for a Hebrew inscription and Star of David on the memorial.

However, X Troop never was a Jewish Commando; it was simply coincidental that many of its exiled German members were Jews by faith, in what was essentially a British Army unit led by a Welsh Presbyterian. As the founder's widow pointed out, Bryan Hilton-Jones did not choose his men for their religion but only for their ability to speak German like a native, and to complete the arduous training of paratrooper commandos. A protestor having no connection with X Troop wrote to Aberdyfi Council condemning the choice of a Saturday – the Jewish Shabat – for the unveiling, saying it would prevent Jews attending. However, the retired American judge who was chairman of the monument committee said: 'The beauty and timelessness of the Welsh slate stone, in its perfect setting, reduces these complaints into insignificance.' The unpleasant acrimony led to the organising committee of five deciding not to hold any religious ceremony during the event.

Bryan Hilton-Jones's widow, Edwina, was one of the committee. They were married in 1943 while she was serving with the Women's Royal Naval Service, at HMS Glendower, the Pwllheli shore base that numbered Prince Philip among its trainees, and later became Butlin's holiday camp. She was born at Llangefni, the daughter of the Reverend Edwin Hughes, later of The Cliff, Caernarfon. After the unveiling of the stone she made a brief speech, in Welsh and English.

The stone commemorates a remarkable unit that never operated as a complete troop, its German-speaking men being temporarily seconded in small groups to other commando units for special operations. The task of discovering the secrets of German anti-invasion devices on the French coast was given to Bryan Hilton-Jones. He took four units of X Troop ashore, in advance of the Allied invasion, and all returned to Britain with invaluable information – a mission for which he was awarded the Military Cross.

Three weeks later Bryan Hilton-Jones and his commandos were back in France and he was severely wounded in the stomach at Caen, and left for dead. A grave had actually been dug for him when he was seen to be recovering and taken to a German field hospital. It was his good fortune that the German doctor was a stomach specialist, and the two men became good friends. With the rapid advance of the British 6th Airborne Division the doctor gave him the option of being abandoned to the hazard of intense British shelling or being taken into captivity. Hilton-Jones took his chance and returned to Britain.

After demobilisation he joined the Foreign Office. Later he joined ICI, becoming managing director first in Ireland, then in Switzerland, and finally in Spain – where he was killed in a car crash on 30 December, 1969. Bryan Hilton-Jones, then aged 51, and his daughter Daryl, 23, were killed instantly. Daughter Nicola, 13, died next day. His wife Edwina, who was also in the car, survived. His son Gavin and third daughter Nerys were in a following car. The family was returning home to Barcelona after a Christmas skiing holiday in Andorra.

Perhaps this book will hand down to posterity the otherwise lost link between the strangely worded Aberdyfi memorial and the great pioneering spirit of the Cofis of Cairo.

Wales' First Lady of Egypt

Mrs Suzanne Mubarak, wife of President Mubarak, of Egypt, is proud of her Welsh background. Her maternal grandfather was a coal miner who worked at several pits in Pontypridd and in the Rhondda Valley, and lived at Trefforest. Her mother, Lily May Palmer, was a nurse at Cardiff Royal Infirmary, where she met and married an Egyptian trainee doctor, before the outbreak of World War II.

Two children, Suzanne and Tony, were born at Minya, the regional capital city south of Cairo. Mrs Mubarak began her education at St Claire's School, Heliopolis, Cairo. She met Muhammad Hosni Mubarak while she was still a student, and he a pilot in the Egyptian Air Force. They were married in 1959. As a mature student she went to Trefforest to study at the local college – her mother's brother John and his wife Lily were then living in Wood Road. Upon her return to Cairo she studied at the city's American University, where she graduated in political science in 1977. Mrs Mubarak received an MA for a sociology thesis in 1982.

President Nasser appointed Hosni Mubarak to chief of staff of the air force in 1969, with the rank of air vice-marshal. President Sadat appointed him commander-in-chief of the air force in 1972, and air marshal in 1974. He was appointed vice-president of Egypt in 1975, and became president after the assassination of Anwar Sadat, in October 1981. One of Mrs Mubarak's first acts, as First Lady of Egypt, was to send for her uncle and aunt, at their terraced house at Trefforest, for a long stay at the Presidential Palace, in Cairo.

As a sociologist, a constant campaigner for women's rights, child protection and literacy, Mrs Mubarak has held several appointments on the world stage. She has two sons and she is a grandmother.

Acknowledgements

Specially written for the 60th anniversary of the Cairo Eisteddfod of 1943, this book has been assembled from information gathered during most of that period, from countless sources. The author particularly wants to record his appreciation of the help and encouragement received since the 1940s from Olwen Hilton-Jones (Caernarfon, daughter of Edward Bryan), William J. Jones (Caernarfon, the first chaired bard of Cairo), T. Elwyn Griffiths (Caeathro, founder editor of *Seren y Dwyrain*), Fred C. Purslow (Coedpoeth, last Welsh owner of Davies Bryan's Cairo shop), Gamal abd an-Nasir (President of Egypt), Siân Wyn Jones (Wrexham, who is writing the definitive history of the Bryan family), Edwina Hilton-Jones (Plymouth, widow of Bryan Hilton-Jones), Adel abd el-Aziz (Cairo, chairman of the Egyptian Tourist Authority), Maha Saad (Cairo, Sheraton/Starwood Hotels), Lady Olwen Carey-Evans (Cricieth, daughter of David Lloyd George), Bruce Jackson (Tyne & Wear Archivist), Berit Scott (London, Royal Norwegian Embassy), Dr Madouh abd el-Zahir (Luxor, retired Inspector of Ancient Monuments), Professor El-Sabahy abd el-Fatah (Cairo, Egyptian Museum), Sabry abd el-Aziz (Luxor, regional manager of West Bank monuments), Neveen el-Halawany Muhammad (Cairo guide), Hassan Ibrahim (Cairo guide), the Right Reverend Ghais abd el-Malik (Bishop of Cairo), Margaret L. Davies (Bala, daughter of the 1943 'bard' Tarw Tura, Dei G. Roberts), Lewis O. Jones (Blaenau Ffestiniog/Rhuthun), Eileen Roberts (Four

Mile Bridge, daughter of Robert Hughes, Cairo), the Reverend Eric Ramage (Beaumaris), Sheikh Mahmoud abd el-Rasul (Gorna) and R. David Hughes (Denbigh).The following publications were useful: *O'r Aifft* (by J.D. Bryan, Wrexham, 1908), *Seren y Dwyrain* (by T. Elwyn Griffiths, Bala, 1955), *The Cairo Parliament* (by Andy Baker, Leigh-on-Sea, 1989), *Pastor on the Nile* (by H.C. Jackson, London, 1960), *Cairo in the War 1939-1945* (by Artemis Cooper, London, 1989), *Return to Oasis* (Selwyn/de Mauny/Fletcher/Fraser/Waller, London, 1980).

Transliterating Arabic into Roman letters always poses problems. In this instance the author has attempted to give the closest proximity to what an Arab actually says, rather than what is usually read in British newspapers. For instance, Faysal indicates the sound better than the conventional spelling Feisal, which is always mispronounced as Fize-al. An Arab says Muhammad, never Mohamed. There are some exceptions in the text: Gamal abd an-Nasir is closest to what an Arab west of Suez would write (those to the east saying Jamal), but few British readers would recognise that for what they are accustomed to seeing as Gamal abd el-Nasser, sometimes Gamal abdel Nasser, or simply Colonel Nasser (or the silly American version Abdul Nasser). In practice many Egyptians say Nasser. The author believes he has used the best Welsh-Arabic compromise (the Welsh having an advantage in such pronunciations as Machmwd for what is always spelt in English as Mahmoud).